GOD'S PROMISES®

for Your Every Need

COUNTRYMAN®

A Division of Thomas Nelson Publishers
Since 1798
www.thomasnelson.com

Compiled by Dr. A.L. Gill.

Library of Congress Cataloging-in-Publication Data

Bible. English. Authorized. Selections. 2006.
God's promises for your every need / [compiled by A.L. Gill].
    p. cm.
ISBN: 1-4041-0410-0 (25th Anniversary Edition, softcover)
ISBN: 1-4041-0411-9 (25th Anniversary Edition, leather)
1. God—Promises—Biblical teaching. 2. Bible—Use.
I. Gill, A. L. II. Title.
BS680.P68B53 2006
220.5'208—dc22

2006000935

Printed in the United States of America

06 07 08 09 10 — 9 8 7 6 5 4 3 2 1

Contents

3. What to Do When You Feel 73

4. What to Do When You Are 113

5. What to Do When 145

6. What the Bible Has to Say About   177

7. Truth from the Bible About   249

Jesus Is Your...

Savior

Not by works of righteousness which we have done, but according to His mercy He saved us, through the washing of regeneration and renewing of the Holy Spirit,

whom He poured out on us abundantly through Jesus Christ our Savior.

Titus 3:5, 6

And we have seen and testify that the Father has sent the Son as Savior of the world.

I John 4:14

And my spirit has rejoiced in God my Savior.

Luke 1:47

For we ourselves have heard Him and we know that this is indeed the Christ, the Savior of the world.

John 4:42b

For the Son of Man has come to seek and to save that which was lost.

Luke 19:10

For God so loved the world that He gave His only begotten Son, that whoever believes in Him should not perish but have everlasting life.

John 3:16

Being justified freely by His grace through the redemption that is in Christ Jesus,

whom God set forth as a propitiation by His blood, through faith, to demonstrate His righteousness, because in His forbearance God had passed over the sins that were previously committed.

Romans 3:24, 25

But God, who is rich in mercy, because of His great love with which He loved us,

even when we were dead in trespasses, made us alive together with Christ (by grace you have been saved).

Ephesians 2:4, 5

Most assuredly, I say to you, he who believes in Me has everlasting life.

John 6:47

For by grace you have been saved through faith, and that not of yourselves; it is the gift of God,

not of works, lest anyone should boast.

Ephesians 2:8, 9

That if you confess with your mouth the Lord Jesus and believe in your heart that God has raised Him from the dead, you will be saved.

Romans 10:9

Therefore, if anyone is in Christ, he is a new creation; old things have passed away; behold, all things have become new.

II Corinthians 5:17

Who has saved us and called us with a holy calling, not according to our works, but according to His own purpose and grace which was given to us in Christ Jesus before time began.

II Timothy 1:9

Nevertheless He saved them for His name's sake, that He might make His mighty power known.

Psalm 106:8

Lord

Therefore God also has highly exalted Him and given Him the name which is above every name,

that at the name of Jesus every knee should bow, of those in heaven, and of those on earth, and of those under the earth,

and that every tongue should confess that Jesus Christ is Lord, to the glory of God the Father.

Philippians 2:9–11

That if you confess with your mouth the Lord Jesus and believe in your heart that God has raised Him from the dead, you will be saved.

For with the heart one believes unto righteousness, and with the mouth confession is made unto salvation.

Romans 10:9, 10

But why do you call Me "Lord, Lord," and not do the things which I say?

Luke 6:46

For sin shall not have dominion over you, for you are not under law but under grace.

What then? Shall we sin because we are not under law but under grace? Certainly not!

Do you not know that to whom you present yourselves slaves to obey, you are that one's slaves whom you obey, whether of sin leading to death, or of obedience leading to righteousness?

Romans 6:14–16

I beseech you therefore, brethren, by the mercies of God, that you present your bodies a living sacrifice, holy, acceptable to God, which is your reasonable service.

And do not be conformed to this world, but be transformed by the renewing of your mind, that you may prove what is that good and acceptable and perfect will of God.

Romans 12:1, 2

Or do you not know that your body is the temple of the Holy Spirit who is in you, whom you have from God, and you are not your own?

For you were bought at a price; therefore glorify God in your body and in your spirit, which are God's.

I Corinthians 6:19, 20

Therefore let all the house of Israel know assuredly that God has made this Jesus, whom you crucified, both Lord and Christ.

Acts 2:36

For if we live, we live to the Lord; and if we die, we die to the Lord. Therefore, whether we live or die, we are the Lord's.

Romans 14:8

Blessed be the Lord,
Who daily loads us with benefits,
The God of our salvation! Selah

Psalm 68:19

But it is good for me to draw near to God;
I have put my trust in the Lord GOD,
That I may declare all your works.

Psalm 73:28

For You, Lord, are good, and ready to forgive,
And abundant in mercy to all those who call upon You.

Psalm 86:5

For the Lord GOD will help Me; therefore I will not be disgraced; therefore I have set My face like a flint, and I know that I will not be ashamed.

Isaiah 50:7

And you shall love the LORD your God with all your heart, with all your soul, with all your mind, and with all your strength. This is the first commandment.

Mark 12:30

For David says concerning Him:
"I foresaw the LORD always before my face,
For He is at my right hand, that I may not be shaken."

Acts 2:25

JESUS IS YOUR
LOVE

But God demonstrates His own love toward us, in that while we were still sinners, Christ died for us.

Romans 5:8

For God so loved the world that He gave His only begotten Son, that whoever believes in Him should not perish but have everlasting life.

John 3:16

Beloved, let us love one another, for love is of God; and everyone who loves is born of God and knows God.

He who does not love does not know God, for God is love.

In this the love of God was manifested toward us, that God has sent His only begotten Son into the world, that we might live through Him.

In this is love, not that we loved God, but that He loved us and sent His Son to be the propitiation for our sins.

Beloved, if God so loved us, we also ought to love one another.

No one has seen God at any time. If we love

one another, God abides in us, and His love has been perfected in us.

1 John 4:7–12

And we have known and believed the love that God has for us. God is love, and he who abides in love abides in God, and God in him.

We love Him because He first loved us.

1 John 4:16, 19

As the Father loved Me, I also have loved you; abide in My love.

If you keep My commandments, you will abide in My love, just as I have kept My Father's commandments and abide in his love.

These things I have spoken to you, that My joy may remain in you, and that your joy may be full.

This is My commandment, that you love one another as I have loved you.

Greater love has no one than this, than to lay down one's life for his friends.

These things I command you, that you love one another.

John 15:9–13, 17

That Christ may dwell in your hearts through faith; that you, being rooted and grounded in love,

may be able to comprehend with all the saints what is the width and length and depth and height—

to know the love of Christ which passes knowledge; that you may be filled with all the fullness of God.

Ephesians 3:17–19

I love those who love me, and those who seek me diligently will find me.

Proverbs 8:17

The LORD has appeared of old to me, saying:
"Yes, I have loved you with an everlasting love;
Therefore with lovingkindness I have drawn you."

Jeremiah 31:3

I will betroth you to Me forever;
Yes, I will betroth you to Me in righteousness and justice,
In lovingkindness and mercy.

Hosea 2:19

He who has My commandments and keeps them, it is he who loves Me. And he who loves Me will be loved by My Father, and I will love him and manifest Myself to him.

John 14:21

The LORD will command his lovingkindness in the daytime,
And in the night His song shall be with me—
A prayer to the God of my life.

Psalm 42:8

And now abide faith, hope, love, these three; but the greatest of these is love.

I Corinthians 13:13

For I am persuaded that neither death nor life, nor angels nor principalities nor powers, nor things present nor things to come,
nor height nor depth, nor any other created thing, shall be able to separate us from the love of God which is in Christ Jesus our Lord.

Romans 8:38, 39

Peace

You will keep him in perfect peace,
Whose mind is stayed on You,
Because he trusts in You.

Isaiah 26:3

But now in Christ Jesus you who once were far off have been brought near by the blood of Christ.

For He Himself is our peace, who has made both one, and has broken down the middle wall of separation.

Ephesians 2:13, 14

Be anxious for nothing, but in everything by prayer and supplication, with thanksgiving, let your requests be made known to God;

and the peace of God, which surpasses all understanding, will guard your hearts and minds through Christ Jesus.

Philippians 4:6, 7

LORD, You will establish peace for us,
For You have also done all our works in us.

Isaiah 26:12

For unto us a Child is born,
Unto us a Son is given;
And the government will be upon His shoulder.
And His name will be called Wonderful,
Counselor,
Mighty God,
Everlasting Father, Prince of Peace.
Of the increase of His government and peace
there will be no end,
Upon the throne of David and over His
kingdom,
To order it and establish it with judgment and
justice from that time forward, even forever.
The zeal of the LORD of hosts will perform
this.

Isaiah 9:6, 7

And the God of peace will crush Satan under
your feet shortly. The grace of our Lord Jesus
Christ be with you. Amen.

Romans 16:20

The things which you learned and received
and heard and saw in me, these do, and the God
of peace will be with you.

Philippians 4:9

Therefore, having been justified by faith, we have peace with God through our Lord Jesus Christ.

Romans 5:1

And let the peace of God rule in your hearts, to which also you were called in one body; and be thankful.

Colossians 3:15

I will both lie down in peace, and sleep;
For You alone, O LORD, make me dwell in safety.

Psalm 4:8

The LORD will give strength to His people;
The LORD will bless His people with peace.

Psalm 29:11

Peace I leave with you, My peace I give to you; not as the world gives do I give to you. Let not your heart be troubled, neither let it be afraid.

John 14:27

Forgiveness

To the praise of the glory of His grace, by which He made us accepted in the Beloved.

In Him we have redemption through His blood, the forgiveness of sins, according to the riches of His grace.

Ephesians 1:6, 7

You have forgiven the iniquity of Your people;
You have covered all their sin. Selah

Psalm 85:2

Therefore, if anyone is in Christ, he is a new creation; old things have passed away; behold, all things have become new.

II Corinthians 5:17

As far as the east is from the west,
So far has He removed our transgressions from us.

Psalm 103:12

My little children, these things I write to you, so that you may not sin. And if anyone sins, we have an Advocate with the Father, Jesus Christ the righteous.

1 John 2:1

If we confess our sins, He is faithful and just to forgive us our sins and to cleanse us from all unrighteousness.

1 John 1:9

For I will be merciful to their unrighteousness, and their sins and their lawless deeds I will remember no more.

Hebrews 8:12

Let the wicked forsake his way,
And the unrighteous man his thoughts;
Let him return to the LORD,
And He will have mercy on him;
And to our God,
For He will abundantly pardon.

Isaiah 55:7

Bearing with one another, and forgiving one another, if anyone has a complaint against another; even as Christ forgave you, so you also must do.

Colossians 3:13

And whenever you stand praying, if you have anything against anyone, forgive him, that your Father in heaven may also forgive you your trespasses.

Mark 11:25

And you, being dead in your trespasses and the uncircumcision of your flesh, He has made alive together with Him, having forgiven you all trespasses.

Colossians 2:13

I will cleanse them from all their iniquity by which they have sinned against Me, and I will pardon all their iniquities by which they have sinned and by which they have transgressed against Me.

Jeremiah 33:8

"Come now, and let us reason together," says the Lord,
"Though your sins are like scarlet,
They shall be as white as snow;
Though they are red like crimson,
They shall be as wool."

Isaiah 1:18

I, even I, am He who blots out your transgressions for My own sake;
And I will not remember your sins.

Isaiah 43:25

Righteousness

For He made Him who knew no sin to be sin for us, that we might become the righteousness of God in Him.

II Corinthians 5:21

But of Him you are in Christ Jesus, who became for us wisdom from God—and righteousness and sanctification and redemption.

I Corinthians 1:30

And be found in Him, not having my own righteousness, which is from the law, but that which is through faith in Christ, the righteousness which is from God by faith.

Philippians 3:9

Just as Abraham "believed God, and it was accounted to him for righteousness."

Therefore know that only those who are of faith are sons of Abraham.

Galatians 3:6, 7

Even the righteousness of God, through faith in Jesus Christ, to all and on all who believe. For there is no difference.

Romans 3:22

Being justified freely by His grace through the redemption that is in Christ Jesus,

whom God set forth as a propitiation by His blood, through faith, to demonstrate His righteousness, because in His forbearance God had passed over the sins that were previously committed,

to demonstrate at the present time His righteousness, that He might be just and the justifier of the one who has faith in Jesus.

Romans 3:24–26

But to him who does not work but believes on Him who justifies the ungodly, his faith is accounted for righteousness.

Romans 4:5

In righteousness you shall be established;
You shall be far from oppression, for you shall not fear;
And from terror, for it shall not come near you.
Indeed they shall surely assemble, but not because of Me.
Whoever assembles against you shall fall for your sake.
"Behold, I have created the blacksmith
Who blows the coals in the fire,
Who brings forth an instrument for his work;
And I have created the spoiler to destroy.

No weapon formed against you shall prosper,
    And every tongue which rises against you in judgment
    You shall condemn.
    This is the heritage of the servants of the LORD,
    And their righteousness is from Me,"
    Says the LORD.

Isaiah 54:14–17

For what the law could not do in that it was weak through the flesh, God did by sending His own Son in the likeness of sinful flesh, on account of sin: He condemned sin in the flesh,
    that the righteous requirement of the law might be fulfilled in us who do not walk according to the flesh but according to the Spirit.

Romans 8:3, 4

For if by the one man's offense death reigned through the one, much more those who receive abundance of grace and of the gift of righteousness will reign in life through the One, Jesus Christ.

Romans 5:17

What shall we say then? That Gentiles, who did not pursue righteousness, have attained to righteousness, even the righteousness of faith.

Romans 9:30

For whom He foreknew, He also predestined to be conformed to the image of His Son, that He might be the firstborn among many brethren.

Moreover whom He predestined, these He also called; whom He called, these He also justified; and whom He justified, these He also glorified.

Romans 8:29, 30

And if Christ is in you, the body is dead because of sin, but the Spirit is life because of righteousness.

Romans 8:10

The work of righteousness will be peace,
And the effect of righteousness, quietness and assurance forever.

Isaiah 32:17

For with the heart one believes unto righteousness, and with the mouth confession is made unto salvation.

Romans 10:10

Not by works of righteousness which we have done, but according to His mercy He saved us, through the washing of regeneration and renewing of the Holy Spirit.

Titus 3:5

Deliverer

The Spirit of the Lord GOD is upon Me,
Because the LORD has anointed Me
To preach good tidings to the poor;
He has sent Me to heal the brokenhearted,
To proclaim liberty to the captives,
And the opening of the prison to those who are bound.

Isaiah 61:1

And you shall know the truth, and the truth shall make you free.
Therefore if the Son makes you free, you shall be free indeed.

John 8:32, 36

For the law of the Spirit of life in Christ Jesus has made me free from the law of sin and death.

Romans 8:2

Behold, I give you the authority to trample on serpents and scorpions, and over all the power of the enemy, and nothing shall by any means hurt you.

Luke 10:19

Now the Lord is the Spirit; and where the Spirit of the Lord is, there is liberty.

II Corinthians 3:17

But now having been set free from sin, and having become slaves of God, you have your fruit to holiness, and the end, everlasting life.

Romans 6:22

For You have broken the yoke of his burden
And the staff of his shoulder,
The rod of his oppressor,
As in the day of Midian.

Isaiah 9:4

The Spirit of the LORD is upon Me,
Because He has anointed Me to preach the gospel to the poor;
He has sent Me to heal the brokenhearted,
To proclaim liberty to the captives
And recovery of sight to the blind,
To set at liberty those who are oppressed.

Luke 4:18

And these signs will follow those who believe: In My name they will cast out demons; they will speak with new tongues.

Mark 16:17

And they overcame him by the blood of the Lamb and by the word of their testimony, and they did not love their lives to the death.

Revelation 12:11

Beloved, do not believe every spirit, but test the spirits, whether they are of God; because many false prophets have gone out into the world.

By this you know the Spirit of God: Every spirit that confesses that Jesus Christ has come in the flesh is of God,

and every spirit that does not confess that Jesus Christ has come in the flesh is not of God. And this is the spirit of the Antichrist, which you have heard was coming, and is now already in the world.

You are of God, little children, and have overcome them, because He who is in you is greater than he who is in the world.

1 John 4:1–4

Fellowship

That which we have seen and heard we declare to you, that you also may have fellowship with us; and truly our fellowship is with the Father and with His Son Jesus Christ.

I John 1:3

God is faithful, by whom you were called into the fellowship of His Son, Jesus Christ our Lord.

I Corinthians 1:9

Behold, I stand at the door and knock. If anyone hears My voice and opens the door, I will come in to him and dine with him, and he with Me.

Revelation 3:20

Jesus answered and said to him, "If anyone loves Me, he will keep My word; and My Father will love him, and We will come to him and make Our home with him."

John 14:23

"Sing and rejoice, O daughter of Zion! For behold, I am coming and I will dwell in your midst," says the LORD.

Zechariah 2:10

For where two or three are gathered together in My name, I am there in the midst of them.

Matthew 18:20

He who has My commandments and keeps them, it is he who loves Me. And he who loves Me will be loved by My Father, and I will love him and manifest Myself to him.

John 14:21

Abide in Me, and I in you. As the branch cannot bear fruit of itself, unless it abides in the vine, neither can you, unless you abide in Me.

I am the vine, you are the branches. He who abides in Me, and I in him, bears much fruit; for without Me you can do nothing.

If you abide in Me, and My words abide in you, you will ask what you desire, and it shall be done for you.

John 15:4, 5, 7

Therefore if there is any consolation in Christ, if any comfort of love, if any fellowship of the Spirit, if any affection and mercy,

fulfill my joy by being like-minded, having the same love, being of one accord, of one mind.

Philippians 2:1, 2

I am a companion of all who fear You, and of those who keep Your precepts.

Psalm 119:63

And walk in love, as Christ also has loved us and given Himself for us, an offering and a sacrifice to God for a sweet-smelling aroma.

Speaking to one another in psalms and hymns and spiritual songs, singing and making melody in your heart to the Lord,

For we are members of His body, of His flesh and of His bones.

Ephesians 5:2, 19, 30

This is the message which we have heard from Him and declare to you, that God is light and in Him is no darkness at all.

If we say that we have fellowship with Him, and walk in darkness, we lie and do not practice the truth.

But if we walk in the light as He is in the light, we have fellowship with one another, and the blood of Jesus Christ His Son cleanses us from all sin.

1 John 1:5–7

Example

For to this you were called, because Christ also suffered for us, leaving us an example, that you should follow His steps.

I Peter 2:21

He who says he abides in Him ought himself also to walk just as He walked.

I John 2:6

Therefore be imitators of God as dear children.

And walk in love, as Christ also has loved us and given Himself for us, an offering and a sacrifice to God for a sweet-smelling aroma.

Ephesians 5:1, 2

Let this mind be in you which was also in Christ Jesus,

who, being in the form of God, did not consider it robbery to be equal with God,

but made Himself of no reputation, taking the form of a bondservant, and coming in the likeness of men.

And being found in appearance as a man, He humbled Himself and became obedient to the point of death, even the death of the cross.

Philippians 2:5–8

Yet it shall not be so among you; but whoever desires to become great among you shall be your servant.

And whoever of you desires to be first shall be slave of all.

For even the Son of Man did not come to be served, but to serve, and to give His life a ransom for many.

Mark 10:43–45

If I then, your Lord and Teacher, have washed your feet, you also ought to wash one another's feet.

For I have given you an example, that you should do as I have done to you.

John 13:14, 15

A new commandment I give to you, that you love one another; as I have loved you, that you also love one another.

John 13:34

By this we know love, because He laid down His life for us. And we also ought to lay down our lives for the brethren.

I John 3:16

Now may the God of patience and comfort grant you to be like-minded toward one another, according to Christ Jesus,

That you may with one mind and one mouth glorify the God and Father of our Lord Jesus Christ.

Therefore receive one another, just as Christ also received us, to the glory of God.

Romans 15:5–7

Bearing with one another, and forgiving one another, if anyone has a complaint against another; even as Christ forgave you, so you also must do.

Colossians 3:13

Looking unto Jesus, the author and finisher of our faith, who for the joy that was set before Him endured the cross, despising the shame, and has sat down at the right hand of the throne of God.

For consider Him who endured such hostility from sinners against Himself, lest you become weary and discouraged in your souls.

Hebrews 12:2, 3

Companion

I am a companion of all who fear You, and of those who keep Your precepts.

Psalm 119:63

A man who has friends must himself be friendly,
But there is a friend who sticks closer than a brother.

Proverbs 18:24

Let your conduct be without covetousness; be content with such things as you have. For He Himself has said, "I will never leave you nor forsake you."

Hebrews 13:5

No longer do I call you servants, for a servant does not know what his master is doing; but I have called you friends; for all things that I heard from My Father I have made known to you.
You did not choose Me, but I chose you and appointed you that you should go and bear fruit, and that your fruit should remain, that whatever you ask the Father in My name He may give you.

John 15:15, 16

But if we walk in the light as He is in the light, we have fellowship with one another, and the blood of Jesus Christ His Son cleanses us from all sin.

I John 1:7

"For the mountains shall depart
And the hills be removed,
But My kindness shall not depart from you,
Nor shall My covenant of peace be removed,"
Says the LORD, who has mercy on you.

Isaiah 54:10

Behold, I stand at the door and knock. If anyone hears My voice and opens the door, I will come in to him and dine with him, and he with Me.

Revelation 3:20

Draw near to God and He will draw near to you. Cleanse your hands, you sinners; and purify your hearts, you double-minded.

James 4:8

When my father and my mother forsake me,
Then the LORD will take care of me.

Psalm 27:10

This is My commandment, that you love one another as I have loved you.

Greater love has no one than this, than to lay down one's life for his friends.

You are My friends if you do whatever I command you.

John 15:12–14

God is faithful, by whom you were called into the fellowship of His Son, Jesus Christ our Lord.

I Corinthians 1:9

That which we have seen and heard we declare to you, that you also may have fellowship with us; and truly our fellowship is with the Father and with His Son Jesus Christ.

I John 1:3

I will not leave you orphans; I will come to you.

John 14:18

Brother

For whoever does the will of My Father in heaven is My brother and sister and mother.

Matthew 12:50

For both He who sanctifies and those who are being sanctified are all of one, for which reason He is not ashamed to call them brethren.

Hebrews 2:11

For whom He foreknew, He also predestined to be conformed to the image of His Son, that He might be the firstborn among many brethren.

Romans 8:29

For you are all sons of God through faith in Christ Jesus.

Galatians 3:26

But as many as received Him, to them He gave the right to become children of God, to those who believe in His name.

John 1:12

Now, therefore, you are no longer strangers and foreigners, but fellow citizens with the saints and members of the household of God.

Ephesians 2:19

Behold what manner of love the Father has bestowed on us, that we should be called children of God! Therefore the world does not know us, because it did not know Him.

I John 3:1

And because you are sons, God has sent forth the Spirit of His Son into your hearts, crying out, "Abba, Father!"

Therefore you are no longer a slave but a son, and if a son, then an heir of God through Christ.

Galatians 4:6, 7

For as many as are led by the Spirit of God, these are sons of God.

Romans 8:14

Beloved, now we are children of God; and it has not yet been revealed what we shall be, but we know that when He is revealed, we shall be like Him, for we shall see Him as He is.

I John 3:2

JESUS IS YOUR
Guardian

When you pass through the waters, I will be with you;
And through the rivers, they shall not overflow you.
When you walk through the fire, you shall not be burned,
Nor shall the flame scorch you.

Isaiah 43:2

But You, O LORD, are a shield for me,
My glory and the One who lifts up my head.

Psalm 3:3

For the eyes of the LORD run to and fro throughout the whole earth, to show Himself strong on behalf of those whose heart is loyal to Him. In this you have done foolishly; therefore from now on you shall have wars.

II Chronicles 16:9a

The LORD your God, who goes before you, He will fight for you, according to all He did for you in Egypt before your eyes.

Deuteronomy 1:30

But the Lord is faithful, who will establish you
and guard you from the evil one.

II Thessalonians 3:3

But if you indeed obey His voice and do all
that I speak, then I will be an enemy to your enemies and an adversary to your adversaries.

Exodus 23:22

He will guard the feet of His saints,
But the wicked shall be silent in darkness.
For by strength no man shall prevail.

I Samuel 2:9

For You have been a shelter for me,
A strong tower from the enemy.

Psalm 61:3

The LORD your God in your midst,
The Mighty One, will save;
He will rejoice over you with gladness,
He will quiet you with his love,
He will rejoice over you with singing.

Zephaniah 3:17

For the eyes of the LORD are on the righteous,
And His ears are open to their prayers;

But the face of the LORD is against those who do evil.

And who is he who will harm you if you become followers of what is good?

I Peter 3:12, 13

The eternal God is your refuge,
And underneath are the everlasting arms;
He will thrust out the enemy from before you,
And will say, "Destroy!"

Deuteronomy 33:27

A thousand may fall at your side,
And ten thousand at your right hand;
But it shall not come near you.

Psalm 91:7

So shall they fear
The name of the LORD from the west,
And His glory from the rising of the sun;
When the enemy comes in like a flood,
The Spirit of the LORD will lift up a standard against him.

Isaiah 59:19

Security

Blessed be the God and Father of our Lord Jesus Christ, who according to His abundant mercy has begotten us again to a living hope through the resurrection of Jesus Christ from the dead,

to an inheritance incorruptible and undefiled and that does not fade away, reserved in heaven for you,

who are kept by the power of God through faith for salvation ready to be revealed in the last time.

I Peter 1:3–5

My sheep hear My voice, and I know them, and they follow Me.

And I give them eternal life, and they shall never perish; neither shall anyone snatch them out of My hand.

My Father, who has given them to Me, is greater than all; and no one is able to snatch them out of My Father's hand.

John 10:27–29

For I am persuaded that neither death nor life, nor angels nor principalities nor powers, nor things present nor things to come, nor height nor depth, nor any other created thing, shall be able to separate us from the love of God which is in Christ Jesus our Lord.

Romans 8:38, 39

Being confident of this very thing, that He who has begun a good work in you will complete it until the day of Jesus Christ.

Philippians 1:6

But the Lord is faithful, who will establish you and guard you from the evil one.

II Thessalonians 3:3

Who also has sealed us and given us the Spirit in our hearts as a guarantee.

II Corinthians 1:22

Now to Him who is able to keep you from stumbling,
And to present you faultless
Before the presence of His glory with exceeding joy,
To God our Savior,
Who alone is wise,
Be glory and majesty,
Dominion and power,
Both now and forever. Amen.

Jude 24, 25

Lift up your eyes on high,
And see who has created these things,
Who brings out their host by number;
He calls them all by name,
By the greatness of His might
And the strength of His power;
Not one is missing.

Isaiah 40:26

Surely goodness and mercy shall follow me
All the days of my life;
And I will dwell in the house of the LORD
Forever.

Psalm 23:6

Do not labor for the food which perishes, but for the food which endures to everlasting life, which the Son of Man will give you, because God the Father has set His seal on Him.

John 6:27

In Him you also trusted, after you heard the word of truth, the gospel of your salvation; in whom also, having believed, you were sealed with the Holy Spirit of promise.

Ephesians 1:13

And do not grieve the Holy Spirit of God, by whom you were sealed for the day of redemption.

Ephesians 4:30

And we desire that each one of you show the same diligence to the full assurance of hope until the end,

that you do not become sluggish, but imitate those who through faith and patience inherit the promises.

that by two immutable things, in which it is impossible for God to lie, we might have strong consolation, who have fled for refuge to lay hold of the hope set before us.

This hope we have as an anchor of the soul, both sure and steadfast, and which enters the Presence behind the veil,

where the forerunner has entered for us, even Jesus, having become High Priest forever according to the order of Melchizedek.

Hebrews 6:11, 12, 18–20

All that the Father gives Me will come to Me, and the one who comes to Me I will by no means cast out.

John 6:37

JESUS IS YOUR
Sufficiency

And God is able to make all grace abound toward you, that you, always having all sufficiency in all things, may have an abundance for every good work.

II Corinthians 9:8

And my God shall supply all your need according to His riches in glory by Christ Jesus.
Philippians 4:19

Therefore I say to you, whatever things you ask when you pray, believe that you receive them, and you will have them.

Mark 11:24

Not that we are sufficient of ourselves to think of anything as being from ourselves, but our sufficiency is from God.

II Corinthians 3:5

I can do all things through Christ who strengthens me.

Philippians 4:13

And what is the exceeding greatness of His power toward us who believe, according to the working of His mighty power.

Ephesians 1:19

And He said to me, "My grace is sufficient for you, for My strength is made perfect in weakness." Therefore most gladly I will rather boast in my infirmities, that the power of Christ may rest upon me.

II Corinthians 12:9

Yet in all these things we are more than conquerors through Him who loved us.

Romans 8:37

Blessed be the God and Father of our Lord Jesus Christ, who has blessed us with every spiritual blessing in the heavenly places in Christ.

Ephesians 1:3

If you abide in Me, and My words abide in you, you will ask what you desire, and it shall be done for you.

John 15:7

And whatever you ask in My name, that I will do, that the Father may be glorified in the Son.

John 14:13

And in that day you will ask Me nothing. Most assuredly, I say to you, whatever you ask the Father in My name He will give you.

Until now you have asked nothing in My name. Ask, and you will receive, that your joy may be full.

John 16:23, 24

And whatever things you ask in prayer, believing, you will receive.

Matthew 21:22

He who did not spare His own Son, but delivered Him up for us all, how shall He not with Him also freely give us all things?

Romans 8:32

As His divine power has given to us all things that pertain to life and godliness, through the knowledge of Him who called us by glory and virtue,

by which have been given to us exceedingly great and precious promises, that through these

you may be partakers of the divine nature, having escaped the corruption that is in the world
through lust.

II Peter 1:3, 4

Bless the LORD, O my soul,
And forget not all His benefits:
Who forgives all your iniquities,
Who heals all your diseases,
Who redeems your life from destruction,
Who crowns you with lovingkindness and
tender mercies.

Psalm 103:2–4

Fulfillment

Blessed are those who hunger and thirst for
righteousness,
  For they shall be filled.

Matthew 5:6

Delight yourself also in the LORD,
And He shall give you the desires of your heart.

Psalm 37:4

For He satisfies the longing soul,
And fills the hungry soul with goodness.

Psalm 107:9

Who satisfies your mouth with good things,
So that your youth is renewed like the eagle's.

Psalm 103:5

You shall eat in plenty and be satisfied,
And praise the name of the LORD your God,
Who has dealt wondrously with you;
And My people shall never be put to shame.

Joel 2:26

And Jesus said to them, "I am the bread of
life. He who comes to Me shall never hunger,
and he who believes in Me shall never thirst."

John 6:35

The poor shall eat and be satisfied;
Those who seek Him will praise the LORD.
Let your heart live forever!

Psalm 22:26

Jesus answered and said to her, "Whoever drinks of this water will thirst again,
"but whoever drinks of the water that I shall give him will never thirst. But the water that I shall give him will become in him a fountain of water springing up into everlasting life."

John 4:13, 14

The LORD will answer and say to His people,
"Behold, I will send you grain and new wine and oil,
And you will be satisfied by them;
I will no longer make you a reproach among the nations."

Joel 2:19

If you extend your soul to the hungry
And satisfy the afflicted soul,
Then your light shall dawn in the darkness,
And your darkness shall be as the noonday.
The LORD will guide you continually,

And satisfy your soul in drought,
And strengthen your bones;
You shall be like a watered garden,
And like a spring of water, whose waters do
not fail.

Isaiah 58:10, 11

The eyes of all look expectantly to You,
And You give them their food in due season.
You open Your hand
And satisfy the desire of every living thing.

Psalm 145:15, 16

Why do you spend money for what is not
bread,
And your wages for what does not satisfy?
Listen carefully to Me, and eat what is good,
And let your soul delight itself in abundance.

Isaiah 55:2

"I will satiate the soul of the priests with
abundance,
And My people shall be satisfied with My
goodness," says the LORD.

Jeremiah 31:14

My soul shall be satisfied as with marrow and
fatness,
And my mouth shall praise You with joyful lips.

When I remember You on my bed,
I meditate on You in the night watches.

Psalm 63:5, 6

He who did not spare His own Son, but delivered Him up for us all, how shall He not with Him also freely give us all things?

Romans 8:32

Everything

And my God shall supply all your need according to His riches in glory by Christ Jesus.
Philippians 4:19

I can do all things through Christ who strengthens me.
Philippians 4:13

Yet in all these things we are more than conquerors through Him who loved us.
Romans 8:37

Therefore let no one boast in men. For all things are yours:
whether Paul or Apollos or Cephas, or the world or life or death, or things present or things to come—all are yours.
And you are Christ's, and Christ is God's.
I Corinthians 3:21–23

Blessed be the Lord,
Who daily loads us with benefits,
The God of our salvation! Selah
Psalm 68:19

And in that day you will ask Me nothing. Most assuredly, I say to you, whatever you ask the Father in My name He will give you.

Until now you have asked nothing in My name. Ask, and you will receive, that your joy may be full.

John 16:23, 24

If you abide in Me, and My words abide in you, you will ask what you desire, and it shall be done for you.

John 15:7

Therefore I say to you, whatever things you ask when you pray, believe that you receive them, and you will have them.

Mark 11:24

Blessed be the God and Father of our Lord Jesus Christ, who has blessed us with every spiritual blessing in the heavenly places in Christ.

Ephesians 1:3

And whatever we ask we receive from Him, because we keep His commandments and do those things that are pleasing in His sight.

I John 3:22

For He made Him who knew no sin to be sin for us, that we might become the righteousness of God in Him.

II Corinthians 5:21

For to me, to live is Christ, and to die is gain.

Philippians 1:21

Therefore, if anyone is in Christ, he is a new creation; old things have passed away; behold, all things have become new.

II Corinthians 5:17

Now to Him who is able to do exceedingly abundantly above all that we ask or think, according to the power that works in us,

To Him be glory in the church by Christ Jesus to all generations, forever and ever. Amen.

Ephesians 3:20, 21

And God is able to make all grace abound toward you, that you, always having all sufficiency in all things, may have an abundance for every good work.

II Corinthians 9:8

And whatever things you ask in prayer, believing, you will receive.

Matthew 21:22

The Bible Is Your...

THE BIBLE IS YOUR
Infallible Authority

· All Scripture is given by inspiration of God,
and is profitable for doctrine, for reproof, for cor-
rection, for instruction in righteousness.

II Timothy 3:16

Knowing this first, that no prophecy of
Scripture is of any private interpretation,
For prophecy never came by the will of man,
but holy men of God spoke as they were moved
by the Holy Spirit.

II Peter 1:20, 21

For the word of God is living and powerful,
and sharper than any two-edged sword, piercing
even to the division of soul and spirit, and of
joints and marrow, and is a discerner of the
thoughts and intents of the heart.

Hebrews 4:12

For as the rain comes down, and the snow
from heaven,
And do not return there,
But water the earth,
And make it bring forth and bud,

That it may give seed to the sower
And bread to the eater,
So shall My word be that goes forth from My
mouth;
It shall not return to Me void,
But it shall accomplish what I please,
And it shall prosper in the thing for which I
sent it.

Isaiah 55:10, 11

You search the Scriptures, for in them you
think you have eternal life; and these are they
which testify of Me.

John 5:39

Having been born again, not of corruptible
seed but incorruptible, through the word of God
which lives and abides forever.

I Peter 1:23

For he spoke, and it was done;
He commanded, and it stood fast.

Psalm 33:9

Every word of God is pure;
He is a shield to those who put their trust in
Him.

Proverbs 30:5

Forever, O LORD,
Your word is settled in heaven.

Psalm 119:89

By the word of the LORD the heavens were made,
And all the host of them by the breath of His mouth.

Psalm 33:6

For all the promises of God in Him are Yes, and in Him Amen, to the glory of God through us.

II Corinthians 1:20

Because "All flesh is as grass,
And all the glory of man as the flower of the grass.
The grass withers,
And its flower falls away,
But the word of the LORD endures forever."

I Peter 1:24, 25

Heaven and earth will pass away, but My words will by no means pass away.

Mark 13:31

Deed of Inheritance

So now, brethren, I commend you to God and to the word of His grace, which is able to build you up and give you an inheritance among all those who are sanctified.

Acts 20:32

To open their eyes, in order to turn them from darkness to light, and from the power of Satan to God, that they may receive forgiveness of sins and an inheritance among those who are sanctified by faith in Me.

Acts 26:18

The Spirit Himself bears witness with our spirit that we are children of God,
And if children, then heirs—heirs of God and joint heirs with Christ, if indeed we suffer with Him, that we may also be glorified together.

Romans 8:16, 17

In Him also we have obtained an inheritance, being predestined according to the purpose of Him who works all things according to the counsel of His will, that we who first trusted in Christ should be to the praise of His glory.

In Him you also trusted, after you heard the word of truth, the gospel of your salvation; in whom also, having believed, you were sealed with the Holy Spirit of promise,

who is the guarantee of our inheritance until the redemption of the purchased possession, to the praise of His glory.

Ephesians 1:11–14

And if you are Christ's, then you are Abraham's seed, and heirs according to the promise.

Galatians 3:29

That the Gentiles should be fellow heirs, of the same body, and partakers of His promise in Christ through the gospel.

Ephesians 3:6

In My Father's house are many mansions; if it were not so, I would have told you. I go to prepare a place for you.

And if I go and prepare a place for you, I will come again and receive you to Myself; that where I am, there you may be also.

John 14:2, 3

But now they desire a better, that is, a heavenly country. Therefore God is not ashamed to be called their God, for He has prepared a city for them.

Hebrews 11:16

Then the King will say to those on His right hand, "Come, you blessed of My Father, inherit the kingdom prepared for you from the foundation of the world."

Matthew 25:34

For all the promises of God in Him are Yes, and in Him Amen, to the glory of God through us.

II Corinthians 1:20

Blessed be the God and Father of our Lord Jesus Christ, who according to His abundant mercy has begotten us again to a living hope through the resurrection of Jesus Christ from the dead,

to an inheritance incorruptible and undefiled and that does not fade away, reserved in heaven for you.

I Peter 1:3, 4

But as it is written:
"Eye has not seen, nor ear heard,

Nor have entered into the heart of man
The things which God has prepared for those
who love Him."

I Corinthians 2:9

By which have been given to us exceedingly
great and precious promises, that through these
you may be partakers of the divine nature, having escaped the corruption that is in the world
through lust.

II Peter 1:4

And whatever you do, do it heartily, as to the
Lord and not to men,
knowing that from the Lord you will receive
the reward of the inheritance; for you serve the
LORD Christ.

Colossians 3:23, 24

Wait on the LORD,
And keep His way,
And He shall exalt you to inherit the land;
When the wicked are cut off, you shall see it.

Psalm 37:34

Guide for Life

Your word is a lamp to my feet
And a light to my path.

Psalm 119:105

When you roam, they will lead you;
When you sleep, they will keep you;
And when you awake, they will speak with you.
For the commandment is a lamp,
And the law a light;
Reproofs of instruction are the way of life.

Proverbs 6:22, 23

Your word I have hidden in my heart,
That I might not sin against You.

Psalm 119:11

Moreover by them Your servant is warned,
And in keeping them there is great reward.

Psalm 19:11

By which have been given to us exceedingly
great and precious promises, that through these you
may be partakers of the divine nature, having escaped
the corruption that is in the world through lust.

II Peter 1:4

How can a young man cleanse his way?
By taking heed according to Your word.

Psalm 119:9

Then Jesus said to those Jews who believed
Him, "If you abide in My word, you are My disciples indeed.
"And you shall know the truth, and the truth
shall make you free."

John 8:31, 32

Your testimonies also are my delight
And my counselors.

Psalm 119:24

The steps of a good man are ordered by the
LORD,
And He delights in his way.

Psalm 37:23

I will instruct you and teach you in the way
you should go;
I will guide you with My eye.

Psalm 32:8

He restores my soul;
He leads me in the paths of righteousness
For His name's sake.

Psalm 23:3

Your ears shall hear a word behind you, say-
ing,
"This is the way, walk in it,"
Whenever you turn to the right hand
Or whenever you turn to the left.
Isaiah 30:21

As He spoke by the mouth of His holy prophets,
Who have been since the world began,
To give light to those who sit in darkness and
the shadow of death,
To guide our feet into the way of peace.
Luke 1:70, 79

This Book of the Law shall not depart from
your mouth, but you shall meditate in it day and
night, that you may observe to do according to
all that is written in it. For then you will make
your way prosperous, and then you will have
good success.

Joshua 1:8

All Scripture is given by inspiration of God,
and is profitable for doctrine, for reproof, for cor-
rection, for instruction in righteousness,
that the man of God may be complete, thor-
oughly equipped for every good work.
II Timothy 3:16, 17

Stability

Having been born again, not of corruptible
seed but incorruptible, through the word of God
which lives and abides forever,
Because "All flesh is as grass,
And all the glory of man as the flower of the grass.
The grass withers,
And its flower falls away,
But the word of the LORD endures forever."
Now this is the word which by the gospel was
preached to you.

I Peter 1:23–25

Forever, O LORD,
Your word is settled in heaven.

Psalm 119:89

Heaven and earth will pass away, but My
words will by no means pass away.

Matthew 24:35

"For I am the LORD. I speak, and the word
which I speak will come to pass; it will no more be
postponed; for in your days, O rebellious house, I will
say the word and perform it,: says the Lord GOD.

Ezekiel 12:25

My son, give attention to my words;
Incline your ear to my sayings.
Do not let them depart from your eyes;
Keep them in the midst of your heart;
For they are life to those who find them,
And health to all their flesh.

Proverbs 4:20–22

The grass withers, the flower fades,
But the word of our God stands forever.

Isaiah 40:8

For assuredly, I say to you, till heaven and earth pass away, one jot or one tittle will by no means pass from the law till all is fulfilled.

Matthew 5:18

Blessed be the LORD, who has given rest to His people Israel, according to all that He promised. There has not failed one word of all His good promise, which He promised through His servant Moses.

I Kings 8:56a

What then shall we say to these things? If God is for us, who can be against us?

Romans 8:31

The eternal God is your refuge,
And underneath are the everlasting arms;

He will thrust out the enemy from before you,
And will say, "Destroy!"

Deuteronomy 33:27

He also brought me up out of a horrible pit,
Out of the miry clay,
And set my feet upon a rock,
And established my steps.

Psalm 40:2

God is our refuge and strength,
A very present help in trouble.

Psalm 46:1

The name of the LORD is a strong tower;
The righteous run to it and are safe.

Proverbs 18:10

But the Lord is faithful, who will establish you
and guard you from the evil one.

II Thessalonians 3:3

Now to Him who is able to keep you from
stumbling, and to present you faultless before the
presence of His glory with exceeding joy,
To God our Savior, who alone is wise, be
glory and majesty, dominion and power, both
now and forever. Amen.

Jude 24, 25

Strength

And he said, "O man greatly beloved, fear not! Peace be to you; be strong, yes, be strong!" So when he spoke to me I was strengthened, and said, "Let my lord speak, for you have strengthened me."

Daniel 10:19

My soul melts from heaviness;
Strengthen me according to Your word.

Psalm 119:28

For thus says the LORD GOD, the Holy One of Israel:
"In returning and rest you shall be saved;
In quietness and confidence shall be your strength."
But you would not.

Isaiah 30:15

That He would grant you, according to the riches of His glory, to be strengthened with might through His Spirit in the inner man,
that Christ may dwell in your hearts through faith; that you, being rooted and grounded in love.

Ephesians 3:16, 17

That you may walk worthy of the Lord, fully pleasing Him, being fruitful in every good work and increasing in the knowledge of God;

strengthened with all might, according to His glorious power, for all patience and longsuffering with joy;

giving thanks to the Father who has qualified us to be partakers of the inheritance of the saints in the light.

Colossians 1:10–12

But those who wait on the LORD
Shall renew their strength;
They shall mount up with wings like eagles,
They shall run and not be weary,
They shall walk and not faint.

Isaiah 40:31

Then he said to them, "Go your way, eat the fat, drink the sweet, and send portions to those for whom nothing is prepared; for this day is holy to our LORD. Do not sorrow, for the joy of the LORD is your strength."

Nehemiah 8:10

I can do all things through Christ who strengthens me.

Philippians 4:13

Fear not, for I am with you;
Be not dismayed, for I am your God.
I will strengthen you,
Yes, I will help you,
I will uphold you with My righteous right hand.

Isaiah 41:10

Counsel is mine, and sound wisdom;
I am understanding, I have strength.

Proverbs 8:14

He gives power to the weak,
And to those who have no might He increases
strength.

Isaiah 40:29

The LORD is my rock and my fortress and
my deliverer;
My God, my strength, in whom I will trust;
My shield and the horn of my salvation, My
stronghold.

Psalm 18:2

Therefore take up the whole armor of God,
that you may be able to withstand in the evil day,
and having done all, to stand.

Ephesians 6:13

The LORD is my light and my salvation; whom shall I fear?
The LORD is the strength of my life;
Of whom shall I be afraid?

Psalm 27:1

Finally, my brethren, be strong in the LORD and in the power of His might.

Ephesians 6:10

What to Do When You Feel...

Discouraged

So the ransomed of the LORD shall return,
And come to Zion with singing,
With everlasting joy on their heads.
They shall obtain joy and gladness;
Sorrow and sighing shall flee away.

Isaiah 51:11

In this you greatly rejoice, though now for a little while, if need be, you have been grieved by various trials,

that the genuineness of your faith, being much more precious than gold that perishes, though it is tested by fire, may be found to praise, honor, and glory at the revelation of Jesus Christ,

whom having not seen you love. Though now you do not see Him, yet believing, you rejoice with joy inexpressible and full of glory,

receiving the end of your faith—the salvation of your souls.

I Peter 1:6–9

Be anxious for nothing, but in everything by prayer and supplication, with thanksgiving, let your requests be made known to God;

and the peace of God, which surpasses all understanding, will guard your hearts and minds through Christ Jesus.

Finally, brethren, whatever things are true, whatever things are noble, whatever things are just, whatever things are pure, whatever things are lovely, whatever things are of good report, if there is any virtue and if there is anything praiseworthy—meditate on these things.

Philippians 4:6–8

Though I walk in the midst of trouble, You will revive me;
You will stretch out your hand
Against the wrath of my enemies,
And Your right hand will save me.

Psalm 138:7

Let not your heart be troubled; you believe in God, believe also in Me.

John 14:1

Peace I leave with you, My peace I give to you; not as the world gives do I give to you. Let not your heart be troubled, neither let it be afraid.

John 14:27

We are hardpressed on every side, yet not crushed; we are perplexed, but not in despair;

Persecuted, but not forsaken; struck down, but not destroyed.

II Corinthians 4:8, 9

Therefore do not cast away your confidence, which has great reward.

For you have need of endurance, so that after you have done the will of God, you may receive the promise.

Hebrews 10:35, 36

Being confident of this very thing, that He who has begun a good work in you will complete it until the day of Jesus Christ.

Philippians 1:6

And let us not grow weary while doing good, for in due season we shall reap if we do not lose heart.

Galatians 6:9

Be of good courage,
And He shall strengthen your heart,
All you who hope in the LORD.

Psalm 31:24

The LORD is my light and my salvation;
Whom shall I fear?
The LORD is the strength of my life;
Of whom shall I be afraid?
When the wicked came against me
To eat up my flesh,
My enemies and foes, they stumbled and fell.
Though an army may encamp against me,
My heart shall not fear;
Though war may rise against me,
In this I will be confident.
One thing I have desired of the LORD,
That will I seek:
That I may dwell in the house of the LORD
All the days of my life,
To behold the beauty of the LORD,
And to inquire in His temple.
For in the time of trouble
He shall hide me in his pavilion;
In the secret place of His tabernacle
He shall hide me;
He shall set me high upon a rock.
And now my head shall be lifted up above
my enemies all around me;
Therefore I will offer sacrifices of joy in His
tabernacle; I will sing, yes,
I will sing praises to the LORD.

Hear, O LORD, when I cry with my voice!
Have mercy also upon me, and answer me.
When You said, "Seek My face,"
My heart said to You, "Your face, LORD, I
will seek."
Do not hide Your face from me;
Do not turn your servant away in anger;
You have been my help;
Do not leave me nor forsake me,
O God of my salvation.
When my father and my mother forsake me,
Then the LORD will take care of me.
Teach me Your way, O LORD,
And lead me in a smooth path, because of
my enemies.
Do not deliver me to the will of my adver-
saries;
For false witnesses have risen against me,
And such as breathe out violence.
I would have lost heart, unless I had believed
That I would see the goodness of the LORD
In the land of the living.
Wait on the LORD;
Be of good courage,
And He shall strengthen your heart;
Wait, I say, on the LORD!

Psalm 27:1–14

Worried

Casting all your care upon Him, for He cares for you.

I Peter 5:7

Let not your heart be troubled; you believe in God, believe also in Me.

John 14:1

Be anxious for nothing, but in everything by prayer and supplication, with thanksgiving, let your requests be made known to God;
And the peace of God, which surpasses all understanding, will guard your hearts and minds through Christ Jesus.

Philippians 4:6, 7

And let the peace of God rule in your hearts, to which also you were called in one body; and be thankful.

Colossians 3:15

You will keep him in perfect peace,
Whose mind is stayed on You,
Because he trusts in You.

Isaiah 26:3

I will both lie down in peace, and sleep;
For You alone, O LORD, make me dwell in safety.

Psalm 4:8

And my God shall supply all your need according to His riches in glory by Christ Jesus.

Philippians 4:19

Therefore I say to you, do not worry about your life, what you will eat or what you will drink; nor about your body, what you will put on. Is not life more than food and the body more than clothing?

Look at the birds of the air, for they neither sow nor reap nor gather into barns; yet your heavenly Father feeds them. Are you not of more value than they?

Which of you by worrying can add one cubit to his stature?

So why do you worry about clothing? Consider the lilies of the field, how they grow: they neither toil nor spin;

and yet I say to you that even Solomon in all his glory was not arrayed like one of these.

Now if God so clothes the grass of the field, which today is, and tomorrow is thrown into the oven, will He not much more clothe you, O you of little faith?

Therefore do not worry, saying, "What shall we eat?" or "What shall we drink?" or "What shall we wear?"

For after all these things the Gentiles seek. For your heavenly Father knows that you need all these things.

But seek first the kingdom of God and His righteousness, and all these things shall be added to you.

Therefore do not worry about tomorrow, for tomorrow will worry about its own things. Sufficient for the day is its own trouble.

Matthew 6:25–34

For to be carnally minded is death, but to be spiritually minded is life and peace.

Romans 8:6

When you lie down, you will not be afraid;
Yes, you will lie down and your sleep will be sweet.

Proverbs 3:24

For we who have believed do enter that rest, as He has said:

"So I swore in My wrath, 'They shall not enter My rest,'"

although the works were finished from the foundation of the world.

There remains therefore a rest for the people of God.

Hebrews 4:3, 9

Great peace have those who love Your law,
And nothing causes them to stumble.

Psalm 119:165

He who dwells in the secret place of the Most High
Shall abide under the shadow of the Almighty.
I will say of the LORD, "He is my refuge and my fortress;
My God, in Him I will trust."

Psalm 91:1, 2

Peace I leave with you, My peace I give to you; not as the world gives do I give to you. Let not your heart be troubled, neither let it be afraid.

John 14:27

Lonely

Let your conduct be without covetousness; be content with such things as you have. For He Himself has said, "I will never leave you nor forsake you."

Hebrews 13:5

Teaching them to observe all things that I have commanded you; and lo, I am with you always, even to the end of the age. Amen.

Matthew 28:20

For the LORD will not forsake His people, for His great name's sake, because it has pleased the LORD to make you His people.

I Samuel 12:22

Fear not, for I am with you;
Be not dismayed, for I am your God.
I will strengthen you,
Yes, I will help you,
I will uphold you with My righteous right hand.

Isaiah 41:10

I will not leave you orphans; I will come to you.

John 14:18

Let not your heart be troubled; you believe in God, believe also in Me.

John 14:1

The eternal God is your refuge,
And underneath are the everlasting arms;
He will thrust out the enemy from before you,
And will say, "Destroy!"

Deuteronomy 33:27

He heals the brokenhearted
And binds up their wounds.

Psalm 147:3

Who shall separate us from the love of Christ? Shall tribulation, or distress, or persecution, or famine, or nakedness, or peril, or sword?

As it is written:

"For Your sake we are killed all day long;
We are accounted as sheep for the slaughter."

Yet in all these things we are more than conquerors through Him who loved us.

For I am persuaded that neither death nor life, nor angels nor principalities nor powers, nor things present nor things to come,

nor height nor depth, nor any other created thing, shall be able to separate us from the love of God which is in Christ Jesus our Lord.

Romans 8:35–39

(For the LORD your God is a merciful God), He will not forsake you nor destroy you, nor forget the covenant of your fathers which He swore to them.

Deuteronomy 4:31

Be strong and of good courage, do not fear nor be afraid of them; for the LORD your God, He is the One who goes with you. He will not leave you nor forsake you."

Deuteronomy 31:6

When my father and my mother forsake me, Then the LORD will take care of me.

Psalm 27:10

"For the mountains shall depart
And the hills be removed,
But My kindness shall not depart from you,
Nor shall My covenant of peace be removed,"
Says the LORD, who has mercy on you.

Isaiah 54:10

Casting all your care upon Him, for He cares for you.

I Peter 5:7

God is our refuge and strength,
A very present help in trouble.

Psalm 46:1

Depressed

The righteous cry out, and the LORD hears,
And delivers them out of all their troubles.
Psalm 34:17

When you pass through the waters, I will be with you;
And through the rivers, they shall not overflow you.
When you walk through the fire, you shall not be burned,
Nor shall the flame scorch you.
Isaiah 43:2

For His anger is but for a moment,
His favor is for life;
Weeping may endure for a night,
But joy comes in the morning.
Psalm 30:5

Beloved, do not think it strange concerning the fiery trial which is to try you, as though some strange thing happened to you;
but rejoice to the extent that you partake of

Christ's sufferings, that when His glory is revealed, you may also be glad with exceeding joy.

I Peter 4:12, 13

To console those who mourn in Zion,
To give them beauty for ashes,
The oil of joy for mourning,
The garment of praise for the spirit of heaviness;
That they may be called trees of righteousness,
The planting of the LORD, that He may be glorified.

Isaiah 61:3

But those who wait on the LORD
Shall renew their strength;
They shall mount up with wings like eagles,
They shall run and not be weary,
They shall walk and not faint.

Isaiah 40:31

Blessed be the God and Father of our Lord Jesus Christ, the Father of mercies and God of all comfort,
who comforts us in all our tribulation, that we may be able to comfort those who are in any

trouble, with the comfort with which we ourselves are comforted by God.

II Corinthians 1:3, 4

For I am persuaded that neither death nor
life, nor angels nor principalities nor powers, nor
things present nor things to come,
nor height nor depth, nor any other created
thing, shall be able to separate us from the love of
God which is in Christ Jesus our Lord.

Romans 8:38, 39

Finally, brethren, whatever things are true,
whatever things are noble, whatever things are
just, whatever things are pure, whatever things
are lovely, whatever things are of good report, if
there is any virtue and if there is anything praiseworthy—meditate on these things.

Philippians 4:8

He heals the brokenhearted
And binds up their wounds.

Psalm 147:3

Fear not, for I am with you;
Be not dismayed, for I am your God.
I will strengthen you,

Yes, I will help you,
I will uphold you with My righteous right hand.

Isaiah 41:10

Therefore humble yourselves under the mighty hand of God, that He may exalt you in due time,
casting all your care upon Him, for He cares for you.

I Peter 5:6, 7

Then he spoke a parable to them, that men always ought to pray and not lose heart.

Luke 18:1

Then he said to them, "Go your way, eat the fat, drink the sweet, and send portions to those for whom nothing is prepared; for this day is holy to our LORD. Do not sorrow, for the joy of the LORD is your strength."

Nehemiah 8:10

So the ransomed of the LORD shall return,
And come to Zion with singing,
With everlasting joy on their heads.
They shall obtain joy and gladness;
Sorrow and sighing shall flee away.

Isaiah 51:11

Dissatisfied

The young lions lack and suffer hunger;
But those who seek the LORD shall not lack
any good thing.

Psalm 34:10

For I will pour water on him who is thirsty,
And floods on the dry ground;
I will pour My Spirit on your descendants,
And My blessing on your offspring.

Isaiah 44:3

Trust in the LORD, and do good;
Dwell in the land, and feed on His faithfulness.

Psalm 37:3

I know how to be abased, and I know how
to abound. Everywhere and in all things I have
learned both to be full and to be hungry, both
to abound and to suffer need.

I can do all things through Christ who
strengthens me.

Philippians 4:12, 13

O God, You are my God;
Early will I seek You;
My soul thirsts for You;
My flesh longs for You
In a dry and thirsty land
Where there is no water.
So I have looked for You in the sanctuary,
To see Your power and Your glory.
Because Your lovingkindness is better than
life,
My lips shall praise You.
Thus I will bless You while I live;
I will lift up my hands in Your name.
My soul shall be satisfied as with marrow and
fatness,
And my mouth shall praise you with joyful
lips.

Psalm 63:1–5

A man will be satisfied with good by the fruit
of his mouth,
And the recompense of a man's hands will be
rendered to him.

Proverbs 12:14

And My people shall be satisfied with My
goodness," says the LORD.

Jeremiah 31:14b

You shall eat in plenty and be satisfied,
And praise the name of the LORD your God,
Who has dealt wondrously with you;
And My people shall never be put to shame.

Joel 2:26

Bless the LORD, O my soul;
And all that is within me, bless His holy name!
Bless the LORD, O my soul,
And forget not all His benefits:
Who forgives all your iniquities,
Who heals all your diseases,
Who redeems your life from destruction,
Who crowns you with lovingkindness and
tender mercies,
Who satisfies your mouth with good things,
So that your youth is renewed like the eagle's.

Psalm 103:1–5

For He satisfies the longing soul,
And fills the hungry soul with goodness.

Psalm 107:9

Behold, God is my salvation,
I will trust and not be afraid;
For YAH, the LORD, is my strength and song;
He also has become my salvation.

Therefore with joy you will draw water
From the wells of salvation.

Isaiah 12:2, 3

And God is able to make all grace abound toward you, that you, always having all sufficiency in all things, may have an abundance for every good work.

II Corinthians 9:8

Ho! Everyone who thirsts,
Come to the waters;
And you who have no money,
Come, buy and eat.
Yes, come, buy wine and milk
Without money and without price.

Isaiah 55:1

Blessed are those who hunger and thirst for righteousness,
For they shall be filled.

Matthew 5:6

Condemned

There is therefore now no condemnation to those who are in Christ Jesus, who do not walk according to the flesh, but according to the Spirit.

Romans 8:1

He has not dealt with us according to our sins,
Nor punished us according to our iniquities.
As far as the east is from the west,
So far has He removed our transgressions from us.

Psalm 103:10, 12

Therefore, if anyone is in Christ, he is a new creation; old things have passed away; behold, all things have become new.

II Corinthians 5:17

For God did not send His Son into the world to condemn the world, but that the world through Him might be saved.

He who believes in Him is not condemned; but he who does not believe is condemned already, because he has not believed in the name of the only begotten Son of God.

John 3:17, 18

Most assuredly, I say to you, he who hears
My word and believes in Him who sent Me has
everlasting life, and shall not come into judgment, but has passed from death into life.

John 5:24

For I will be merciful to their unrighteousness, and their sins and their lawless deeds I will
remember no more.

Hebrews 8:12

I, even I, am He who blots out your transgressions for My own sake; and I will not remember your sins.

Isaiah 43:25

Let the wicked forsake his way,
And the unrighteous man his thoughts;
Let him return to the LORD, and
He will have mercy on him;
And to our God,
For He will abundantly pardon.

Isaiah 55:7

I acknowledged my sin to You,
And my iniquity I have not hidden.

I said, "I will confess my transgressions to the LORD,"

And You forgave the iniquity of my sin. Selah

Psalm 32:5

If we confess our sins, He is faithful and just to forgive us our sins and to cleanse us from all unrighteousness.

I John 1:9

Blessed is he whose transgression is forgiven, Whose sin is covered.

Psalm 32:1

Then I heard a loud voice saying in heaven, "Now salvation, and strength, and the kingdom of our God, and the power of His Christ have come, for the accuser of our brethren, who accused them before our God day and night, has been cast down.

And they overcame him by the blood of the Lamb and by the word of their testimony, and they did not love their lives to the death."

Revelation 12:10, 11

When Jesus had raised Himself up and saw no one but the woman, He said to her, "Woman, where are those accusers of yours? Has no one condemned you?"

She said, "No one, Lord." And Jesus said to her, "Neither do I condemn you; go and sin no more."

John 8:10, 11

"No more shall every man teach his neighbor, and every man his brother, saying, 'Know the LORD,' for they all shall know Me, from the least of them to the greatest of them," says the LORD. "For I will forgive their iniquity, and their sin I will remember no more."

Jeremiah 31:34

Let us draw near with a true heart in full assurance of faith, having our hearts sprinkled from an evil conscience and our bodies washed with pure water.

Hebrews 10:22

For if you return to the LORD, your brethren and your children will be treated with compassion by those who lead them captive, so that they may come back to this land; for the LORD your God is gracious and merciful, and will not turn His face from you if you return to Him.

II Chronicles 30:9

Confused

For God is not the author of confusion but of peace, as in all the churches of the saints.

I Corinthians 14:33

For God has not given us a spirit of fear, but of power and of love and of a sound mind.

II Timothy 1:7

For where envy and self-seeking exist, confusion and every evil thing are there.

But the wisdom that is from above is first pure, then peaceable, gentle, willing to yield, full of mercy and good fruits, without partiality and without hypocrisy.

Now the fruit of righteousness is sown in peace by those who make peace.

James 3:16–18

For the Lord GOD will help Me;
Therefore I will not be disgraced;
Therefore I have set My face like a flint,
And I know that I will not be ashamed.

Isaiah 50:7

Beloved, do not think it strange concerning the fiery trial which is to try you, as though some strange thing happened to you;

but rejoice to the extent that you partake of Christ's sufferings, that when His glory is revealed, you may also be glad with exceeding joy.

I Peter 4:12, 13

If any of you lacks wisdom, let him ask of God, who gives to all liberally and without reproach, and it will be given to him.

James 1:5

Trust in the LORD with all your heart,
And lean not on your own understanding;
In all your ways acknowledge Him,
And He shall direct your paths.

Proverbs 3:5, 6

I will instruct you and teach you in the way you should go;
I will guide you with My eye.

Psalm 32:8

Great peace have those who love Your law,
And nothing causes them to stumble.

Psalm 119:165

Cast your burden on the LORD,
And He shall sustain you;
He shall never permit the righteous to be moved.

Psalm 55:22

When you pass through the waters, I will be with you;
And through the rivers, they shall not overflow you.
When you walk through the fire, you shall not be burned,
Nor shall the flame scorch you.

Isaiah 43:2

He gives power to the weak,
And to those who have no might He increases strength.

Isaiah 40:29

Your ears shall hear a word behind you, saying,
"This is the way, walk in it,"
Whenever you turn to the right hand
Or whenever you turn to the left.

Isaiah 30:21

Be anxious for nothing, but in everything by prayer and supplication, with thanksgiving, let your requests be made known to God;
and the peace of God, which surpasses all understanding, will guard your hearts and minds through Christ Jesus.

Philippians 4:6, 7

Tempted

Therefore let him who thinks he stands take heed lest he fall.

No temptation has overtaken you except such as is common to man; but God is faithful, who will not allow you to be tempted beyond what you are able, but with the temptation will also make the way of escape, that you may be able to bear it.

I Corinthians 10:12, 13

Seeing then that we have a great High Priest who has passed through the heavens, Jesus the Son of God, let us hold fast our confession.

For we do not have a High Priest who cannot sympathize with our weaknesses, but was in all points tempted as we are, yet without sin.

Let us therefore come boldly to the throne of grace, that we may obtain mercy and find grace to help in time of need.

Hebrews 4:14–16

For in that He Himself has suffered, being tempted, He is able to aid those who are tempted.

Hebrews 2:18

Then the Lord knows how to deliver the godly out of temptations.

II Peter 2:9a

For sin shall not have dominion over you, for you are not under law but under grace.

Romans 6:14

Your word I have hidden in my heart,
That I might not sin against You.

Psalm 119:11

Let no one say when he is tempted, "I am tempted by God"; for God cannot be tempted by evil, nor does He Himself tempt anyone.
But each one is tempted when he is drawn away by his own desires and enticed.

James 1:13, 14

He who covers his sins will not prosper,
But whoever confesses and forsakes them will have mercy.

Proverbs 28:13

If we confess our sins, He is faithful and just to forgive us our sins and to cleanse us from all unrighteousness.

I John 1:9

Be sober, be vigilant; because your adversary the devil walks about like a roaring lion, seeking whom he may devour.

Resist him, steadfast in the faith, knowing that the same sufferings are experienced by your brotherhood in the world.

I Peter 5:8, 9

Finally, my brethren, be strong in the Lord and in the power of His might.

Put on the whole armor of God, that you may be able to stand against the wiles of the devil.

above all, taking the shield of faith with which you will be able to quench all the fiery darts of the wicked one.

Ephesians 6:10, 11, 16

Therefore submit to God. Resist the devil and he will flee from you.

James 4:7

You are of God, little children, and have over-come them, because He who is in you is greater than he who is in the world.

I John 4:4

My brethren, count it all joy when you fall into various trials,

Knowing that the testing of your faith produces patience.

Blessed is the man who endures temptation; for when he has been approved, he will receive the crown of life which the Lord has promised to those who love Him.

James 1:2, 3, 12

Now to Him who is able to keep you from stumbling,

And to present you faultless

Before the presence of His glory with exceeding joy,

To God our Savior,

Who alone is wise,

Be glory and majesty.

Jude 24, 25a

In this you greatly rejoice, though now for a little while, if need be, you have been grieved by various trials,

That the genuineness of your faith, being much more precious than gold that perishes, though it is tested by fire, may be found to praise, honor, and glory at the revelation of Jesus Christ.

I Peter 1:6, 7

Angry

So then, my beloved brethren, let every man be swift to hear, slow to speak, slow to wrath;

for the wrath of man does not produce the righteousness of God.

James 1:19, 20

"Be angry, and do not sin": do not let the sun go down on your wrath.

Ephesians 4:26

A soft answer turns away wrath,
But a harsh word stirs up anger.

Proverbs 15:1

For if you forgive men their trespasses, your heavenly Father will also forgive you.

Matthew 6:14

He who is slow to wrath has great understanding,
But he who is impulsive exalts folly.

Proverbs 14:29

Cease from anger, and forsake wrath;
Do not fret—it only causes harm.

Psalm 37:8

He who is slow to anger is better than the mighty,
And he who rules his spirit than he who takes a city.

Proverbs 16:32

Do not hasten in your spirit to be angry,
For anger rests in the bosom of fools.

Ecclesiastes 7:9

Beloved, do not avenge yourselves, but rather give place to wrath; for it is written, "Vengeance is Mine, I will repay," says the Lord.

Romans 12:19

If your enemy is hungry, give him bread to eat;
And if he is thirsty, give him water to drink;
For so you will heap coals of fire on his head,
And the LORD will reward you.

Proverbs 25:21, 22

For we know him who said, "Vengeance is mine, I will repay," says the Lord. And again, "The LORD will judge His people."

Hebrews 10:30

Let all bitterness, wrath, anger, clamor, and evil speaking be put away from you, with all malice.

And be kind to one another, tenderhearted, forgiving one another, even as God in Christ forgave you.

Ephesians 4:31, 32

But I say to you that whoever is angry with his brother without a cause shall be in danger of the judgment. And whoever says to his brother, 'Raca!' shall be in danger of the council. But whoever says, 'You fool!' shall be in danger of hell fire.

Therefore if you bring your gift to the altar, and there remember that your brother has something against you,

leave your gift there before the altar, and go your way. First be reconciled to your brother, and then come and offer your gift.

Matthew 5:22–24

A wise man fears and departs from evil,
But a fool rages and is self-confident.
A quick-tempered man acts foolishly,
And a man of wicked intentions is hated.

Proverbs 14:16, 17

But now you yourselves are to put off all these: anger, wrath, malice, blasphemy, filthy language out of your mouth.

Colossians 3:8

Rebellious

Obey those who rule over you, and be submissive, for they watch out for your souls, as those who must give account. Let them do so with joy and not with grief, for that would be unprofitable for you.

Hebrews 13:17

A wise man fears and departs from evil,
But a fool rages and is self-confident.
A quick-tempered man acts foolishly,
And a man of wicked intentions is hated.

Proverbs 14:16, 17

So Samuel said:
"Has the LORD as great delight in burnt offerings and sacrifices,
As in obeying the voice of the LORD?
Behold, to obey is better than sacrifice,
And to heed than the fat of rams.
For rebellion is as the sin of witchcraft,
And stubbornness is as iniquity and idolatry.
Because you have rejected the word of the LORD,
He also has rejected you from being king."

I Samuel 15:22, 23

Therefore gird up the loins of your mind, be sober, and rest your hope fully upon the grace that is to be brought to you at the revelation of Jesus Christ;

as obedient children, not conforming yourselves to the former lusts, as in your ignorance.

I Peter 1:13, 14

If you are willing and obedient,
You shall eat the good of the land;
But if you refuse and rebel,
You shall be devoured by the sword;
For the mouth of the LORD has spoken.

Isaiah 1:19, 20

Therefore submit yourselves to every ordinance of man for the Lord's sake, whether to the king as supreme,

or to governors, as to those who are sent by him for the punishment of evildoers and for the praise of those who do good.

For this is the will of God, that by doing good you may put to silence the ignorance of foolish men.

I Peter 2:13–15

Let this mind be in you which was also in Christ Jesus,

who, being in the form of God, did not consider it robbery to be equal with God,

but made Himself of no reputation, taking the form of a bondservant, and coming in the likeness of men.

And being found in appearance as a man, He humbled Himself and became obedient to the point of death, even the death of the cross.

Philippians 2:5–8

Though He was a Son, yet He learned obedience by the things which he suffered.

Hebrews 5:8

Likewise you younger people, submit yourselves to your elders. Yes, all of you be submissive to one another, and be clothed with humility, for

"God resists the proud,

But gives grace to the humble."

Therefore humble yourselves under the mighty hand of God, that He may exalt you in due time.

I Peter 5:5, 6

Submitting to one another in the fear of God.

Ephesians 5:21

No grave trouble will overtake the righteous, But the wicked shall be filled with evil.

Proverbs 12:21

Therefore do not let sin reign in your mortal body, that you should obey it in its lusts.

And do not present your members as instruments of unrighteousness to sin, but present yourselves to God as being alive from the dead, and your members as instruments of righteousness to God.

Romans 6:12, 13

This I say, therefore, and testify in the Lord, that you should no longer walk as the rest of the Gentiles walk, in the futility of their mind,

having their understanding darkened, being alienated from the life of God, because of the ignorance that is in them, because of the blindness of their heart.

Ephesians 4:17, 18

For you were once darkness, but now you are light in the Lord. Walk as children of light.

Ephesians 5:8

Therefore submit to God. Resist the devil and he will flee from you.

James 4:7

What to Do When You Are...

Experiencing Fear

For God has not given us a spirit of fear, but of power and of love and of a sound mind.

II Timothy 1:7

For you did not receive the spirit of bondage again to fear, but you received the Spirit of adoption by whom we cry out, "Abba, Father."

Romans 8:15

There is no fear in love; but perfect love casts out fear, because fear involves torment. But he who fears has not been made perfect in love.

I John 4:18

He who dwells in the secret place of the Most High shall abide under the shadow of the Almighty.

Psalm 91:1

He shall cover you with His feathers,
And under His wings you shall take refuge;
His truth shall be your shield and buckler.
You shall not be afraid of the terror by night,
Nor of the arrow that flies by day,
Nor of the pestilence that walks in darkness,
Nor of the destruction that lays waste at noonday.

A thousand may fall at your side,
And ten thousand at your right hand;
But it shall not come near you.

Psalm 91:4–7

No evil shall befall you,
Nor shall any plague come near your dwelling;
For He shall give his angels charge over you,
To keep you in all your ways.

Psalm 91:10, 11

Do not be afraid of sudden terror,
Nor of trouble from the wicked when it comes;
For the LORD will be your confidence,
And will keep your foot from being caught.

Proverbs 3:25, 26

In righteousness you shall be established;
You shall be far from oppression, for you shall
not fear;
And from terror, for it shall not come near you.

Isaiah 54:14

In God I have put my trust;
I will not be afraid.
What can man do to me?

Psalm 56:11

Yea, though I walk through the valley of the shadow of death,

I will fear no evil;

For You are with me;

Your rod and Your staff, they comfort me.

You prepare a table before me in the presence of my enemies;

You anoint my head with oil; my cup runs over.

Psalm 23:4, 5

For whom He foreknew, He also predestined to be conformed to the image of his Son, that He might be the firstborn among many brethren.

What then shall we say to these things? If God is for us, who can be against us?

Who shall separate us from the love of Christ? Shall tribulation, or distress, or persecution, or famine, or nakedness, or peril, or sword?

As it is written:

"For Your sake we are killed all day long;

We are accounted as sheep for the slaughter."

Yet in all these things we are more than conquerors through Him who loved us.

For I am persuaded that neither death nor life, nor angels nor principalities nor powers, nor things present nor things to come,

nor height nor depth, nor any other created

thing, shall be able to separate us from the love of God which is in Christ Jesus our Lord.

Romans 8:29, 31, 35–39

Be of good courage,
And He shall strengthen your heart,
All you who hope in the LORD.

Psalm 31:24

Peace I leave with you, my peace I give to you; not as the world gives do I give to you. Let not your heart be troubled, neither let it be afraid.

John 14:27

The LORD is my light and my salvation;
Whom shall I fear?
The LORD is the strength of my life;
Of whom shall I be afraid?
Though an army may encamp against me,
My heart shall not fear;
Though war may rise against me,
In this I will be confident.

Psalm 27:1, 3

So we may boldly say:
"The LORD is my helper;
I will not fear.
What can man do to me?"

Hebrews 13:6

Mentally Disturbed

For God has not given us a spirit of fear, but of power and of love and of a sound mind.

II Timothy 1:7

Fear not, for I am with you;
Be not dismayed, for I am your God.
I will strengthen you,
Yes, I will help you,
I will uphold you with My righteous right hand.

Isaiah 41:10

For God is not the author of confusion but of peace.

I Corinthians 14:33a

For where envy and self-seeking exist, confusion and every evil thing are there.

But the wisdom that is from above is first pure, then peaceable, gentle, willing to yield, full of mercy and good fruits, without partiality and without hypocrisy.

Now the fruit of righteousness is sown in peace by those who make peace.

James 3:16–18

Therefore it is also contained in the Scripture,
"Behold, I lay in Zion
A chief cornerstone, elect, precious,
And he who believes on Him will by no means
be put to shame."

I Peter 2:6

"For the LORD GOD will help Me;
Therefore I will not be disgraced;
Therefore I have set My face like a flint,
And I know that I will not be ashamed.

Isaiah 50:7

Cast your burden on the LORD
And He shall sustain you;
He shall never permit the righteous to be
moved.

Psalm 55:22

Be anxious for nothing, but in everything by
prayer and supplication, with thanksgiving, let
your requests be made known to God;
and the peace of God, which surpasses all
understanding, will guard your hearts and minds
through Christ Jesus.

Philippians 4:6, 7

Great peace have those who love Your law,
And nothing causes them to stumble.

Psalm 119:165

For his anger is but for a moment,
His favor is for life;
Weeping may endure for a night,
But joy comes in the morning.

Psalm 30:5

When you pass through the waters, I will be
with you;
And through the rivers, they shall not overflow you.
When you walk through the fire, you shall
not be burned,
Nor shall the flame scorch you.

Isaiah 43:2

He heals the brokenhearted
And binds up their wounds.

Psalm 147:3

Blessed be the God and Father of our Lord
Jesus Christ, the Father of mercies and God of all
comfort,
who comforts us in all our tribulation, that

we may be able to comfort those who are in any trouble, with the comfort with which we ourselves are comforted by God.

II Corinthians 1:3, 4

Finally, brethren, whatever things are true, whatever things are noble, whatever things are just, whatever things are pure, whatever things are lovely, whatever things are of good report, if there is any virtue and if there is anything praiseworthy—meditate on these things.

Philippians 4:8

For I am persuaded that neither death nor life, nor angels nor principalities nor powers, nor things present nor things to come,

nor height nor depth, nor any other created thing, shall be able to separate us from the love of God which is in Christ Jesus our Lord.

Romans 8:38, 39

In Need of Courage

Wait on the LORD;
Be of good courage,
And He shall strengthen your heart;
Wait, I say, on the LORD!

Psalm 27:14

For his anger is but for a moment,
His favor is for life;
Weeping may endure for a night,
But joy comes in the morning.

Psalm 30:5

When you pass through the waters, I will be
with you;
And through the rivers, they shall not overflow you.
When you walk through the fire, you shall
not be burned,
Nor shall the flame scorch you.

Isaiah 43:2

Beloved, do not think it strange concerning
the fiery trial which is to try you, as though some
strange thing happened to you;

but rejoice to the extent that you partake of Christ's sufferings, that when His glory is revealed, you may also be glad with exceeding joy.

I Peter 4:12, 13

For I am persuaded that neither death nor life, nor angels nor principalities nor powers, nor things present nor things to come,

nor height nor depth, nor any other created thing, shall be able to separate us from the love of God which is in Christ Jesus our Lord.

Romans 8:38, 39

Fear not, for I am with you;
Be not dismayed, for I am your God.
I will strengthen you,
Yes, I will help you,
I will uphold you with My righteous right hand.

Isaiah 41:10

The eternal God is your refuge,
And underneath are the everlasting arms;
He will thrust out the enemy from before you,
And will say, 'Destroy!'

Deuteronomy 33:27

I shall not die, but live,
And declare the works of the LORD.

Psalm 118:17

I can do all things through Christ who strengthens me.

Philippians 4:13

Be of good courage,
And He shall strengthen your heart,
All you who hope in the LORD.

Psalm 31:24

But those who wait on the LORD
Shall renew their strength;
They shall mount up with wings like eagles,
They shall run and not be weary,
They shall walk and not faint.

Isaiah 40:31

Be anxious for nothing, but in everything by prayer and supplication, with thanksgiving, let your requests be made known to God.

Philippians 4:6

Finally, brethren, whatever things are true, whatever things are noble, whatever things are just, whatever things are pure, whatever things are lovely, whatever things are of good report, if there is any virtue and if there is anything praiseworthy—meditate on these things.

Philippians 4:8

So the ransomed of the LORD shall return,
And come to Zion with singing,
With everlasting joy on their heads.
They shall obtain joy and gladness;
Sorrow and sighing shall flee away.

Isaiah 51:11

In Need of Patience

But the fruit of the Spirit is love, joy, peace, longsuffering, kindness, goodness, faithfulness.

Galatians 5:22

But those who wait on the LORD
Shall renew their strength;
They shall mount up with wings like eagles,
They shall run and not be weary,
They shall walk and not faint.

Isaiah 40:31

Wait on the LORD;
Be of good courage,
And He shall strengthen your heart;
Wait, I say, on the LORD!

Psalm 27:14

It is good that one should hope and wait quietly
For the salvation of the LORD.

Lamentations 3:26

But if we hope for what we do not see, we eagerly wait for it with perseverance.

Romans 8:25

Rest in the LORD, and wait patiently for Him;
Do not fret because of him who prospers in his way,
Because of the man who brings wicked schemes to pass.

Psalm 37:7

That you do not become sluggish, but imitate those who through faith and patience inherit the promises.

Hebrews 6:12

Therefore do not cast away your confidence, which has great reward.

For you have need of endurance, so that after you have done the will of God, you may receive the promise:

"For yet a little while,
And He who is coming will come and will not tarry."

Hebrews 10:35–37

Therefore we also, since we are surrounded by so great a cloud of witnesses, let us lay aside every weight, and the sin which so easily ensnares us, and let us run with endurance the race that is set before us.

Hebrews 12:1

The end of a thing is better than its beginning;
The patient in spirit is better than the proud
in spirit.
Do not hasten in your spirit to be angry,
For anger rests in the bosom of fools.

Ecclesiastes 7:8, 9

For whatever things were written before were
written for our learning, that we through the
patience and comfort of the Scriptures might
have hope.
Now may the God of patience and comfort
grant you to be like-minded toward one another,
according to Christ Jesus.

Romans 15:4, 5

Cease from anger, and forsake wrath;
Do not fret—it only causes harm.
For evildoers shall be cut off;
But those who wait on the LORD,
They shall inherit the earth.

Psalm 37:8, 9

I waited patiently for the LORD;
And He inclined to me, and heard my cry.

Psalm 40:1

And not only that, but we also glory in tribulations, knowing that tribulation produces perseverance;

and perseverance, character; and character, hope.

Now hope does not disappoint, because the love of God has been poured out in our hearts by the Holy Spirit who was given to us.

Romans 5:3–5

Knowing that the testing of your faith produces patience.

But let patience have its perfect work, that you may be perfect and complete, lacking nothing.

James 1:3, 4

Therefore be patient, brethren, until the coming of the Lord. See how the farmer waits for the precious fruit of the earth, waiting patiently for it until it receives the early and latter rain.

You also be patient. Establish your hearts, for the coming of the Lord is at hand.

James 5:7, 8

In Need of Peace

You will keep him in perfect peace,
Whose mind is stayed on You,
Because he trusts in You.

Isaiah 26:3

Peace I leave with you, My peace I give to you; not as the world gives do I give to you. Let not your heart be troubled, neither let it be afraid.

John 14:27

Be anxious for nothing, but in everything by prayer and supplication, with thanksgiving, let your requests be made known to God;
and the peace of God, which surpasses all understanding, will guard your hearts and minds through Christ Jesus.

Philippians 4:6, 7

Therefore, having been justified by faith, we have peace with God through our Lord Jesus Christ.

Romans 5:1

LORD , You will establish peace for us,
For You have also done all our works in us.

Isaiah 26:12

For you shall go out with joy,
And be led out with peace;
The mountains and the hills
Shall break forth into singing before you,
And all the trees of the field shall clap their hands.

Isaiah 55:12

Mark the blameless man, and observe the upright;
For the future of that man is peace.

Psalm 37:37

For to be carnally minded is death, but to be spiritually minded is life and peace.

Romans 8:6

Great peace have those who love Your law,
And nothing causes them to stumble.

Psalm 119:165

He shall enter into peace;
They shall rest in their beds,
Each one walking in his uprightness.

Isaiah 57:2

For the kingdom of God is not eating and drinking, but righteousness and peace and joy in the Holy Spirit.

For he who serves Christ in these things is acceptable to God and approved by men.

Therefore let us pursue the things which make for peace and the things by which one may edify another.

Romans 14:17–19

But the meek shall inherit the earth,
And shall delight themselves in the abundance of peace.

Psalm 37:11

Finally, brethren, farewell. Become complete. Be of good comfort, be of one mind, live in peace; and the God of love and peace will be with you.

II Corinthians 13:11

Now may the God of hope fill you with all joy and peace in believing, that you may abound in hope by the power of the Holy Spirit.

Romans 15:13

Lukewarm Spiritually

Be watchful, and strengthen the things which remain, that are ready to die, for I have not found your works perfect before God.

I know your works, that you are neither cold nor hot. I could wish you were cold or hot.

So then, because you are lukewarm, and neither cold nor hot, I will vomit you out of My mouth.

Revelation 3:2, 15, 16

Nevertheless I have this against you, that you have left your first love.

Revelation 2:4

O Ephraim, what shall I do to you?
O Judah, what shall I do to you?
For your faithfulness is like a morning cloud,
And like the early dew it goes away.

Hosea 6:4

Only take heed to yourself, and diligently keep yourself, lest you forget the things your eyes have seen, and lest they depart from your heart all the days of your life. And teach them to your children and your grandchildren.

Deuteronomy 4:9

Beware that you do not forget the LORD your God by not keeping His commandments, His judgments, and His statutes which I command you today,

lest—when you have eaten and are full, and have built beautiful houses and dwell in them;

and when your herds and your flocks multiply, and your silver and your gold are multiplied, and all that you have is multiplied;

when your heart is lifted up, and you forget the LORD your God who brought you out of the land of Egypt, from the house of bondage.

Deuteronomy 8:11–14

If we had forgotten the name of our God,
Or stretched out our hands to a foreign god,
Would not God search this out?
For He knows the secrets of the heart.

Psalm 44:20, 21

Beware, brethren, lest there be in any of you an evil heart of unbelief in departing from the living God;

but exhort one another daily, while it is called "Today," lest any of you be hardened through the deceitfulness of sin.

Hebrews 3:12, 13

Of whom we have much to say, and hard to explain, since you have become dull of hearing.

For though by this time you ought to be teachers, you need someone to teach you again the first principles of the oracles of God; and you have come to need milk and not solid food.

Hebrews 5:11, 12

Looking carefully lest anyone fall short of the grace of God; lest any root of bitterness springing up cause trouble, and by this many become defiled.

Hebrews 12:15

For if, after they have escaped the pollutions of the world through the knowledge of the Lord and Savior Jesus Christ, they are again entangled in them and overcome, the latter end is worse for them than the beginning.

For it would have been better for them not to have known the way of righteousness, than having known it, to turn from the holy commandment delivered to them.

II Peter 2:20, 21

Thus says the LORD:
"Stand in the ways and see,
And ask for the old paths, where the good way is,
And walk in it;
Then you will find rest for your souls.
But they said, 'We will not walk in it.'"

Jeremiah 6:16

If we confess our sins, He is faithful and just to forgive us our sins and to cleanse us from all unrighteousness.

I John 1:9

"Yet from the days of your fathers
You have gone away from My ordinances
And have not kept them.
Return to Me, and I will return to you,"
Says the LORD of hosts.

Malachi 3:7a

In Grief

But I do not want you to be ignorant, brethren, concerning those who have fallen asleep, lest you sorrow as others who have no hope.

For if we believe that Jesus died and rose again, even so God will bring with Him those who sleep in Jesus.

I Thessalonians 4:13, 14

For the LORD has comforted His people,
And will have mercy on His afflicted.

Isaiah 49:13b

When you pass through the waters, I will be with you;
And through the rivers, they shall not overflow you.
When you walk through the fire, you shall not be burned,
Nor shall the flame scorch you.

Isaiah 43:2

Now may our Lord Jesus Christ Himself, and our God and Father, who has loved us and given us everlasting consolation and good hope by grace, comfort your hearts and establish you in every good word and work.

II Thessalonians 2:16, 17

Blessed are those who mourn,
For they shall be comforted.

Matthew 5:4

Blessed be the God and Father of our Lord Jesus Christ, the Father of mercies and God of all comfort,

who comforts us in all our tribulation, that we may be able to comfort those who are in any trouble, with the comfort with which we ourselves are comforted by God.

II Corinthians 1:3, 4

The Spirit of the Lord GOD is upon Me,
Because the LORD has anointed Me
To preach good tidings to the poor;
He has sent Me to heal the brokenhearted,
To proclaim liberty to the captives,
And the opening of the prison to those who are bound;
To proclaim the acceptable year of the LORD
And the day of vengeance of our God;
To comfort all who mourn,
To console those who mourn in Zion,

To give them beauty for ashes,
The oil of joy for mourning,
The garment of praise for the spirit of heaviness;
That they may be called trees of righteousness,
the planting of the LORD, that He may be glorified.

Isaiah 61:1–3

This is my comfort in my affliction,
For Your word has given me life.

Psalm 119:50

Casting all your care upon Him, for He cares for you.

I Peter 5:7

"O Death, where is your sting?
O Hades, where is your victory?"
The sting of death is sin, and the strength of sin is the law.
But thanks be to God, who gives us the victory through our Lord Jesus Christ.

I Corinthians 15:55–57

Yea, though I walk through the valley of the shadow of death,
I will fear no evil;
For You are with me;
Your rod and Your staff, they comfort me.

Psalm 23:4

For we do not have a High Priest who cannot sympathize with our weaknesses, but was in all points tempted as we are, yet without sin.

Let us therefore come boldly to the throne of grace, that we may obtain mercy and find grace to help in time of need.

Hebrews 4:15, 16

Fear not, for I am with you;
Be not dismayed, for I am your God.
I will strengthen you,
Yes, I will help you,
I will uphold you with My righteous right hand.

Isaiah 41:10

So the ransomed of the LORD shall return,
And come to Zion
With singing, with everlasting joy on their heads.
They shall obtain joy and gladness;
Sorrow and sighing shall flee away.

Isaiah 51:11

We are confident, yes, well pleased rather to be absent from the body and to be present with the Lord.

II Corinthians 5:8

And God will wipe away every tear from their eyes; there shall be no more death, nor sorrow, nor crying. There shall be no more pain, for the former things have passed away.

Revelation 21:4

In Doubt About God

So Jesus answered and said to them, "Have faith in God.

"For assuredly, I say to you, whoever says to this mountain, 'Be removed and be cast into the sea,' and does not doubt in his heart, but believes that those things he says will be done, he will have whatever he says.

"Therefore I say to you, whatever things you ask when you pray, believe that you receive them, and you will have them."

Mark 11:22–24

And do not seek what you should eat or what you should drink, nor have an anxious mind.

For all these things the nations of the world seek after, and your Father knows that you need these things.

But seek the kingdom of God, and all these things shall be added to you.

Luke 12:29–31

He did not waver at the promise of God through unbelief, but was strengthened in faith, giving glory to God, and being fully convinced that what He had promised He was also able to perform.

Romans 4:20, 21

My counsel shall stand,
And I will do all My pleasure,
Indeed I have spoken it;
I will also bring it to pass.
I have purposed it;
I will also do it.

Isaiah 46:10b, 11b

He who calls you is faithful, who also will do it.

I Thessalonians 5:24

The Lord is not slack concerning His promise, as some count slackness, but is longsuffering toward us, not willing that any should perish but that all should come to repentance.

II Peter 3:9

So then faith comes by hearing, and hearing by the word of God.

Romans 10:17

Behold, the LORD's hand is not shortened,
That it cannot save;
Nor His ear heavy,
That it cannot hear.

Isaiah 59:1

Beloved, do not think it strange concerning the fiery trial which is to try you, as though some strange thing happened to you;

but rejoice to the extent that you partake of Christ's sufferings, that when His glory is revealed, you may also be glad with exceeding joy.

I Peter 4:12, 13

For as the rain comes down, and the snow from heaven,
And do not return there,
But water the earth,
And make it bring forth and bud,
That it may give seed to the sower
And bread to the eater,
So shall My word be that goes forth from My mouth;
It shall not return to Me void,
But it shall accomplish what I please,
And it shall prosper in the thing for which I sent it.

Isaiah 55:10, 11

What to Do When...

WHAT TO DO WHEN
You Need Confidence

I can do all things through Christ who strengthens me.

Philippians 4:13

So we may boldly say:
"The LORD is my helper;
I will not fear.
What can man do to me?"

Hebrews 13:6

Therefore do not cast away your confidence, which has great reward.

For you have need of endurance, so that after you have done the will of God, you may receive the promise.

Hebrews 10:35, 36

Being confident of this very thing, that He who has begun a good work in you will complete it until the day of Jesus Christ.

Philippians 1:6

The LORD God is my strength;
He will make my feet like deer's feet,
And He will make me walk on my high hills.

Habakkuk 3:19

Yet in all these things we are more than conquerors through Him who loved us.

Romans 8:37

Now this is the confidence that we have in Him, that if we ask anything according to His will, He hears us.

And if we know that He hears us, whatever we ask, we know that we have the petitions that we have asked of Him.

I John 5:14, 15

Most assuredly, I say to you, He who believes in Me, the works that I do He will do also; and greater works than these He will do, because I go to my Father.

John 14:12

So he answered and said to me:
"This is the word of the LORD to Zerubbabel:
'Not by might nor by power, but by my spirit,'
Says the LORD of hosts."

Zechariah 4:6

When you pass through the waters, I will be with you;

And through the rivers, they shall not overflow you.

When you walk through the fire, you shall
not be burned,
Nor shall the flame scorch you.

Isaiah 43:2

For the L ORD will be your confidence,
And will keep your foot from being caught.

Proverbs 3:26

Therefore I rejoice that I have confidence in
you in everything.

II Corinthians 7:16

In whom we have boldness and access with
confidence through faith in Him.

Ephesians 3:12

Beloved, if our heart does not condemn us,
we have confidence toward God.

I John 3:21

But those who wait on the L ORD
Shall renew their strength;
They shall mount up with wings like eagles,
They shall run and not be weary,
They shall walk and not faint.

Isaiah 40:31

Troubles Hit Your Life

The Lord is good,
A stronghold in the day of trouble;
And He knows those who trust in Him.

Nahum 1:7

We are hard-pressed on every side, yet not crushed; we are perplexed, but not in despair;
persecuted, but not forsaken; struck down, but not destroyed.

II Corinthians 4:8, 9

Though I walk in the midst of trouble,
You will revive me;
You will stretch out Your hand
Against the wrath of my enemies,
And Your right hand will save me.

Psalm 138:7

Let not your heart be troubled; you believe in God, believe also in Me.

John 14:1

When you pass through the waters, I will be with you;
And through the rivers, they shall not overflow you.

When you walk through the fire, you shall not be burned,
Nor shall the flame scorch you.

Isaiah 43:2

And we know that all things work together for good to those who love God, to those who are the called according to His purpose.

Romans 8:28

I will be glad and rejoice in your mercy,
For You have considered my trouble;
You have known my soul in adversities.

Psalm 31:7

I will lift up my eyes to the hills—
From whence comes my help?
My help comes from the LORD,
Who made heaven and earth.

Psalm 121:1, 2

For we do not have a High Priest who cannot sympathize with our weaknesses, but was in all points tempted as we are, yet without sin.
Let us therefore come boldly to the throne of grace, that we may obtain mercy and find grace to help in time of need.

Hebrews 4:15, 16

Casting all your care upon Him, for He cares for you.

I Peter 5:7

Therefore do not worry about tomorrow, for tomorrow will worry about its own things. Sufficient for the day is its own trouble.

Matthew 6:34

Blessed be the God and Father of our Lord Jesus Christ, the Father of mercies and God of all comfort,

who comforts us in all our tribulation, that we may be able to comfort those who are in any trouble, with the comfort with which we ourselves are comforted by God.

II Corinthians 1:3, 4

Be anxious for nothing, but in everything by prayer and supplication, with thanksgiving, let your requests be made known to God;

and the peace of God, which surpasses all understanding, will guard your hearts and minds through Christ Jesus.

Philippians 4:6, 7

You Have a Physical Sickness

Beloved, I pray that you may prosper in all things and be in health, just as your soul prospers.

III John 2

Then Jesus went about all the cities and villages, teaching in their synagogues, preaching the gospel of the kingdom, and healing every sickness and every disease among the people.

Matthew 9:35

And the whole multitude sought to touch Him, for power went out from Him and healed them all.

Luke 6:19

Jesus Christ is the same yesterday, today, and forever.

Hebrews 13:8

Who Himself bore our sins in His own body on the tree, that we, having died to sins, might live for righteousness—by whose stripes you were healed.

I Peter 2:24

Who forgives all your iniquities,
Who heals all your diseases.

Psalm 103:3

But He was wounded for our transgressions,
He was bruised for our iniquities;
The chastisement for our peace was upon Him,
And by His stripes we are healed.

Isaiah 53:5

Heal me, O LORD, and I shall be healed;
Save me, and I shall be saved,
For You are my praise.

Jeremiah 17:14

"For I will restore health to you
And heal you of your wounds," says the LORD.

Jeremiah 30:17a

If you diligently heed the voice of the LORD
your God and do what is right in His sight, give
ear to His commandments and keep all His
statutes, I will put none of the diseases on you
which I have brought on the Egyptians. For I am
the LORD who heals you.

Exodus 15:26

My son, give attention to my words;
Incline your ear to my sayings.

Do not let them depart from your eyes;
Keep them in the midst of your heart;
For they are life to those who find them,
And health to all their flesh.

Proverbs 4:20–22

He sent His word and healed them,
And delivered them from their destructions.

Psalm 107:20

The centurion answered and said, "Lord, I am not worthy that you should come under my roof. But only speak a word, and my servant will be healed."

Matthew 8:8

Is anyone among you sick? Let him call for the elders of the church, and let them pray over him, anointing him with oil in the name of the Lord.

And the prayer of faith will save the sick, and the Lord will raise him up. And if he has committed sins, he will be forgiven.

James 5:14, 15

And these signs will follow those who believe: In My name they will cast out demons; they will speak with new tongues;

they will take up serpents; and if they drink anything deadly, it will by no means hurt them; they will lay hands on the sick, and they will recover.

Mark 16:17, 18

When You Are in Financial Trouble

Beloved, I pray that you may prosper in all things and be in health, just as your soul prospers.

III John 2

I have been young, and now am old;
Yet I have not seen the righteous forsaken,
Nor his descendants begging bread.

Psalm 37:25

The young lions lack and suffer hunger;
But those who seek the LORD shall not lack any good thing.

Psalm 34:10

The LORD is my shepherd;
I shall not want.

Psalm 23:1

And all these blessings shall come upon you and overtake you, because you obey the voice of the LORD your God:

"Blessed shall you be in the city, and blessed shall you be in the country.

"Blessed shall be the fruit of your body, the produce of your ground and the increase of your herds, the increase of your cattle and the offspring of your flocks.

"Blessed shall be your basket and your kneading bowl.

"Blessed shall you be when you come in, and blessed shall you be when you go out.

"The LORD will cause your enemies who rise against you to be defeated before your face; they shall come out against you one way and flee before you seven ways.

"The LORD will command the blessing on you in your storehouses and in all to which you set your hand, and He will bless you in the land which the LORD your God is giving you."

Deuteronomy 28:2–8

And the LORD will grant you plenty of goods, in the fruit of your body, in the increase of your livestock, and in the produce of your ground, in the land of which the LORD swore to your fathers to give you.

The LORD will open to you His good treasure, the heavens, to give the rain to your land in its season, and to bless all the work of your hand. You shall lend to many nations, but you shall not borrow.

And the LORD will make you the head and not

the tail; you shall be above only, and not be beneath, if you heed the commandments of the LORD your God, which I command you today, and are careful to observe them.

Deuteronomy 28:11–13

Give, and it will be given to you: good measure, pressed down, shaken together, and running over will be put into your bosom. For with the same measure that you use, it will be measured back to you.

Luke 6:38

On the first day of the week let each one of you lay something aside, storing up as he may prosper, that there be no collections when I come.

I Corinthians 16:2

Heal the sick, cleanse the lepers, raise the dead, cast out demons. Freely you have received, freely give.

Matthew 10:8

"Bring all the tithes into the storehouse,
That there may be food in My house,
And try Me now in this," says the LORD of hosts,
"if I will not open for you the windows of heaven

And pour out for you such blessing

That there will not be room enough to receive it.

"And I will rebuke the devourer for your sakes,

So that he will not destroy the fruit of your ground,

Nor shall the vine fail to bear fruit for you in the field,"

Says the Lord of hosts;

"And all nations will call you blessed,

For you will be a delightful land,"

Says the Lord of hosts.

Malachi 3:10–12

But this I say: He who sows sparingly will also reap sparingly, and he who sows bountifully will also reap bountifully.

So let each one give as he purposes in his heart, not grudgingly or of necessity; for God loves a cheerful giver.

And God is able to make all grace abound toward you, that you, always having all sufficiency in all things, may have an abundance for every good work.

II Corinthians 9:6–8

And everyone who has left houses or brothers or sisters or father or mother or wife or children or lands, for My name's sake, shall receive a hundredfold, and inherit eternal life.

Matthew 19:29

This Book of the Law shall not depart from your mouth, but you shall meditate in it day and night, that you may observe to do according to all that is written in it. For then you will make your way prosperous, and then you will have good success.

Joshua 1:8

For God gives wisdom and knowledge and joy to a man who is good in His sight; but to the sinner He gives the work of gathering and collecting, that he may give to him who is good before God. This also is vanity and grasping for the wind.

Ecclesiastes 2:26

A good man leaves an inheritance to his children's children,
But the wealth of the sinner is stored up for the righteous.

Proverbs 13:22

For the LORD your God is bringing you into a good land, a land of brooks of water, of fountains and springs, that flow out of valleys and hills;

a land of wheat and barley, of vines and fig trees and pomegranates, a land of olive oil and honey;

a land in which you will eat bread without scarcity, in which you will lack nothing; a land whose stones are iron and out of whose hills you can dig copper.

When you have eaten and are full, then you shall bless the LORD your God for the good land which He has given you.

Beware that you do not forget the LORD your God by not keeping His commandments, His judgments, and His statutes which I command you today,

lest—when you have eaten and are full, and have built beautiful houses and dwell in them;

and when your herds and your flocks multiply, and your silver and your gold are multiplied, and all that you have is multiplied;

when your heart is lifted up, and you forget the Lord your God who brought you out of the land of Egypt, from the house of bondage;

And you shall remember the LORD your God, for it is He who gives you power to get wealth, that He may establish His covenant which He swore to your fathers, as it is this day.

Deuteronomy 8:7–14, 18

Therefore do not worry, saying, "What shall we eat?" or "What shall we drink?" or "What shall we wear?"

For after all these things the Gentiles seek. For your heavenly Father knows that you need all these things.

But seek first the kingdom of God and His righteousness, and all these things shall be added to you.

Matthew 6:31–33

And my God shall supply all your need according to His riches in glory by Christ Jesus.

Philippians 4:19

You Are Having Marital Problems

Let all bitterness, wrath, anger, clamor, and evil speaking be put away from you, with all malice.

And be kind to one another, tenderhearted, forgiving one another, even as God in Christ forgave you.

Ephesians 4:31, 32

And the LORD God said, "It is not good that man should be alone; I will make him a helper comparable to him."

Genesis 2:18

Therefore a man shall leave his father and mother and be joined to his wife, and they shall become one flesh.

Genesis 2:24

Submitting to one another in the fear of God.

Wives, submit to your own husbands, as to the Lord.

For the husband is head of the wife, as also Christ is head of the church; and He is the Savior of the body.

Therefore, just as the church is subject to Christ, so let the wives be to their own husbands in everything.

Husbands, love your wives, just as Christ also loved the church and gave Himself for her,

that he might sanctify and cleanse her with the washing of water by the word,

that He might present her to Himself a glorious church, not having spot or wrinkle or any such thing, but that she should be holy and without blemish.

So husbands ought to love their own wives as their own bodies; he who loves his wife loves himself.

For no one ever hated his own flesh, but nourishes and cherishes it, just as the Lord does the church.

For we are members of His body, of His flesh and of His bones.

"For this reason a man shall leave his father and mother and be joined to his wife, and the two shall become one flesh."

This is a great mystery, but I speak concerning Christ and the church.

Nevertheless let each one of you in particular so love his own wife as himself, and let the wife see that she respects her husband.

Ephesians 5:21–33

Wives, likewise, be submissive to your own husbands, that even if some do not obey the word, they, without a word, may be won by the conduct of their wives,

when they observe your chaste conduct accompanied by fear.

Do not let your adornment be merely outward—arranging the hair, wearing gold, or putting on fine apparel—

rather let it be the hidden person of the heart, with the incorruptible beauty of a gentle and quiet spirit, which is very precious in the sight of God.

For in this manner, in former times, the holy women who trusted in God also adorned themselves, being submissive to their own husbands,

as Sarah obeyed Abraham, calling him lord, whose daughters you are if you do good and are not afraid with any terror.

Husbands, likewise, dwell with them with understanding, giving honor to the wife, as to the weaker vessel, and as being heirs together of the grace of life, that your prayers may not be hindered.

I Peter 3:1–7

And if it seems evil to you to serve the Lord, choose for yourselves this day whom you will serve, whether the gods which your fathers served that were on the other side of the River, or the gods of the Amorites, in whose land you dwell. But as for me and my house, we will serve the LORD.

Joshua 24:15

Love does no harm to a neighbor; therefore love is the fulfillment of the law.

Romans 13:10

I will behave wisely in a perfect way.
Oh, when will You come to me?
I will walk within my house with a perfect heart.

Psalm 101:2

Finally, all of you be of one mind, having compassion for one another; love as brothers, be tenderhearted, be courteous;
not returning evil for evil or reviling for reviling, but on the contrary blessing, knowing that you were called to this, that you may inherit a blessing.
For He who would love life
And see good days,
Let him refrain his tongue from evil,
And his lips from speaking deceit.

Let him turn away from evil and do good;
Let him seek peace and pursue it.

I Peter 3:8–11

Trust in the LORD with all your heart,
And lean not on your own understanding;
In all your ways acknowledge Him,
And He shall direct your paths.

Proverbs 3:5, 6

Hatred stirs up strife,
But love covers all sins.

Proverbs 10:12

Since you have purified your souls in obeying the truth through the spirit in sincere love of
the brethren, love one another fervently with a
pure heart.

I Peter 1:22

You Are Deserted By Loved Ones

And those who know your name will put their trust in You;

For You, LORD, have not forsaken those who seek You.

Psalm 9:10

For the LORD will not cast off His people, Nor will He forsake His inheritance.

Psalm 94:14

When my father and my mother forsake me, Then the LORD will take care of me.

Psalm 27:10

Teaching them to observe all things that I have commanded you; and lo, I am with you always, even to the end of the age. Amen.

Matthew 28:20

You shall no longer be termed Forsaken, Nor shall your land any more be termed Desolate;

But you shall be called Hephzibah, and your land Beulah;

For the LORD delights in you,
And your land shall be married.

Isaiah 62:4

Persecuted, but not forsaken; struck down, but not destroyed.

II Corinthians 4:9

Casting all your care upon Him, for He cares for you.

I Peter 5:7

I have been young, and now am old;
Yet I have not seen the righteous forsaken,
Nor his descendants begging bread.

Psalm 37:25

(For the Lord your God is a merciful God), He will not forsake you nor destroy you, nor forget the covenant of your fathers which He swore to them.

Deuteronomy 4:31

The poor and needy seek water, but there is none,
Their tongues fail for thirst.
I, the LORD, will hear them;
I, the God of Israel, will not forsake them.

Isaiah 41:17

Because he has set his love upon Me, therefore
I will deliver him;
I will set him on high, because he has known
My name.
He shall call upon Me, and I will answer him;
I will be with him in trouble;
I will deliver him and honor him.

Psalm 91:14, 15

Can a woman forget her nursing child,
And not have compassion on the son of her
womb?
Surely they may forget,
Yet I will not forget you.
See, I have inscribed you on the palms of My
hands;
Your walls are continually before Me.

Isaiah 49:15, 16

Why are you cast down, O my soul?
And why are you disquieted within me?
Hope in God;
For I shall yet praise Him,
The help of my countenance and my God.

Psalm 43:5

Be strong and of good courage, do not fear
nor be afraid of them; for the LORD your God,

He is the One who goes with you. He will not leave you nor forsake you.

Deuteronomy 31:6

For the LORD will not forsake His people, for His great name's sake, because it has pleased the LORD to make you His people.

I Samuel 12:22

You Do Not Understand God's Ways

"For My thoughts are not your thoughts,
Nor are your ways My ways," says the LORD.
"For as the heavens are higher than the earth,
So are My ways higher than your ways,
And My thoughts than your thoughts."

Isaiah 55:8, 9

Call to Me, and I will answer you, and show you great and mighty things, which you do not know.

Jeremiah 33:3

What then shall we say to these things? If God is for us, who can be against us?

Romans 8:31

Who shall separate us from the love of Christ? Shall tribulation, or distress, or persecution, or famine, or nakedness, or peril, or sword?
As it is written:
"For Your sake we are killed all day long;
We are accounted as sheep for the slaughter."

Yet in all these things we are more than conquerors through Him who loved us.

Romans 8:35–37

No temptation has overtaken you except such as is common to man; but God is faithful, who will not allow you to be tempted beyond what you are able, but with the temptation will also make the way of escape, that you may be able to bear it.

I Corinthians 10:13

Many are the afflictions of the righteous,
But the LORD delivers him out of them all.

Psalm 34:19

Cast your burden on the Lord,
And He shall sustain you;
He shall never permit the righteous to be moved.

Psalm 55:22

Fear not, for I am with you;
Be not dismayed, for I am your God.
I will strengthen you,
Yes, I will help you,

I will uphold you with My righteous right hand.

Isaiah 41:10

And we know that all things work together for good to those who love God, to those who are the called according to His purpose.

Romans 8:28

Let us know,
Let us pursue the knowledge of the LORD.
His going forth is established as the morning;
He will come to us like the rain,
Like the latter and former rain to the earth.

Hosea 6:3

As for God, His way is perfect;
The word of the LORD is proven;
He is a shield to all who trust in Him.

Psalm 18:30

Let us hold fast the confession of our hope without wavering, for He who promised is faithful.

Hebrews 10:23

And I will make an everlasting covenant with them, that I will not turn away from doing them good; but I will put My fear in their hearts so that they will not depart from Me.

Jeremiah 32:40

The Lord will perfect that which concerns me;
Your mercy, O LORD, endures forever;
Do not forsake the works of Your hands.

Psalm 138:8

Beloved, do not think it strange concerning the fiery trial which is to try you, as though some strange thing happened to you;
but rejoice to the extent that you partake of Christ's sufferings, that when His glory is revealed, you may also be glad with exceeding joy.

I Peter 4:12, 13

You Are Waiting on God

Wait on the LORD;
Be of good courage,
And He shall strengthen your heart;
Wait, I say, on the LORD!

Psalm 27:14

My soul, wait silently for God alone,
For my expectation is from Him.

Psalm 62:5

Our soul waits for the LORD;
He is our help and our shield.

Psalm 33:20

But those who wait on the LORD
Shall renew their strength;
They shall mount up with wings like eagles,
They shall run and not be weary,
They shall walk and not faint.

Isaiah 40:31

For the vision is yet for an appointed time;
But at the end it will speak, and it will not lie.
Though it tarries, wait for it;

Because it will surely come,
It will not tarry.

Habakkuk 2:3

Let us hold fast the confession of our hope without wavering, for He who promised is faithful.

Hebrews 10:23

The eyes of all look expectantly to You,
And You give them their food in due season.
You open Your hand
And satisfy the desire of every living thing.

Psalm 145:15, 16

I wait for the LORD, my soul waits,
And in His word I do hope.

Psalm 130:5

For we have become partakers of Christ if we hold the beginning of our confidence steadfast to the end.

Hebrews 3:14

What the Bible
Has to Say About...

Faith

Now faith is the substance of things hoped for, the evidence of things not seen.

Hebrews 11:1

So then faith comes by hearing, and hearing by the word of God.

Romans 10:17

For I say, through the grace given to me, to everyone who is among you, not to think of himself more highly than he ought to think, but to think soberly, as God has dealt to each one a measure of faith.

Romans 12:3

Looking unto Jesus, the author and finisher of our faith, who for the joy that was set before Him endured the cross, despising the shame, and has sat down at the right hand of the throne of God.

Hebrews 12:2

So Jesus said to them, "Because of your unbelief; for assuredly, I say to you, if you have faith as a mustard seed, you will say to this mountain, 'Move from here to there,' and it will move; and nothing will be impossible for you."

Matthew 17:20

So Jesus answered and said to them, "Have faith in God.

"For assuredly, I say to you, whoever says to this mountain, 'Be removed and be cast into the sea,' and does not doubt in his heart, but believes that those things he says will be done, he will have whatever he says.

"Therefore I say to you, whatever things you ask when you pray, believe that you receive them, and you will have them."

Mark 11:22–24

For in it the righteousness of God is revealed from faith to faith; as it is written, "The just shall live by faith."

Romans 1:17

For we walk by faith, not by sight.

II Corinthians 5:7

But without faith it is impossible to please Him, for He who comes to God must believe that

He is, and that He is a rewarder of those who diligently seek Him.

Hebrews 11:6

That the genuineness of your faith, being much more precious than gold that perishes, though it is tested by fire, may be found to praise, honor, and glory at the revelation of Jesus Christ,

whom having not seen you love. Though now you do not see him, yet believing, you rejoice with joy inexpressible and full of glory,

receiving the end of your faith—the salvation of your souls.

I Peter 1:7–9

For whatever is born of God overcomes the world. And this is the victory that has overcome the world—our faith.

I John 5:4

And suddenly, a woman who had a flow of blood for twelve years came from behind and touched the hem of His garment.

For she said to herself, "If only I may touch His garment, I shall be made well."

But Jesus turned around, and when He saw her He said, "Be of good cheer, daughter; your faith has made you well." And the woman was made well from that hour.

Matthew 9:20–22

And when He had come into the house, the blind men came to Him. And Jesus said to them, "Do you believe that I am able to do this?" They said to him, "Yes, LORD."

Then He touched their eyes, saying, "According to your faith let it be to you."

Matthew 9:28, 29

Jesus said to him, "If you can believe, all things are possible to him who believes."

Mark 9:23

Is anyone among you sick? Let him call for the elders of the church, and let them pray over him, anointing him with oil in the name of the Lord.

And the prayer of faith will save the sick, and the LORD will raise him up.

James 5:14, 15a

Love

Beloved, let us love one another, for love is of God; and everyone who loves is born of God and knows God.

He who does not love does not know God, for God is love.

I John 4:7, 8

Though I speak with the tongues of men and of angels, but have not love, I have become sounding brass or a clanging cymbal.

And though I have the gift of prophecy, and understand all mysteries and all knowledge, and though I have all faith, so that I could remove mountains, but have not love, I am nothing.

And though I bestow all my goods to feed the poor, and though I give my body to be burned, but have not love, it profits me nothing.

Love suffers long and is kind; love does not envy; love does not parade itself, is not puffed up;

does not behave rudely, does not seek its own, is not provoked, thinks no evil;

does not rejoice in iniquity, but rejoices in the truth;

bears all things, believes all things, hopes all things, endures all things.

Love never fails.

And now abide faith, hope, love, these three; but the greatest of these is love.

I Corinthians 13:1–8a, 13

In this is love, not that we loved God, but that He loved us and sent His Son to be the propitiation for our sins.

Beloved, if God so loved us, we also ought to love one another.

No one has seen God at any time. If we love one another, God abides in us, and His love has been perfected in us.

I John 4:10–12

As the Father loved Me, I also have loved you; abide in My love.

If you keep My commandments, you will abide in My love, just as I have kept My Father's commandments and abide in His love.

John 15:9, 10

He who has My commandments and keeps them, it is he who loves Me. And he who loves Me will be loved by My Father, and I will love him and manifest Myself to him.

John 14:21

This is My commandment, that you love one another as I have loved you.

Greater love has no one than this, than to lay down one's life for his friends.

You are My friends if you do whatever I command you.

These things I command you, that you love one another.

John 15:12–14, 17

"And you shall love the LORD your God with all your heart, with all your soul, with all your mind, and with all your strength." This is the first commandment.

And the second, like it, is this: "You shall love your neighbor as yourself." There is no other commandment greater than these.

And to love Him with all the heart, with all the understanding, with all the soul, and with all the strength, and to love one's neighbor as oneself, is more than all the whole burnt offerings and sacrifices.

Mark 12:30, 31, 33

And we have known and believed the love that God has for us. God is love, and he who abides in love abides in God, and God in him.

And this commandment we have from Him:
that he who loves God must love his brother also.
I John 4:16, 21

The LORD has appeared of old to me, saying:
"Yes, I have loved you with an everlasting love;
Therefore with lovingkindness I have drawn
you."

Jeremiah 31:3

For the Father Himself loves you, because you
have loved Me, and have believed that I came forth
from God.

John 16:27

But God demonstrates His own love toward
us, in that while we were still sinners, Christ died
for us.

Romans 5:8

For God so loved the world that He gave His
only begotten Son, that whoever believes in Him
should not perish but have everlasting life.

John 3:16

For I am persuaded that neither death nor
life, nor angels nor principalities nor powers, nor
things present nor things to come,

nor height nor depth, nor any other created thing, shall be able to separate us from the love of God which is in Christ Jesus our Lord.

Romans 8:38, 39

A new commandment I give to you, that you love one another; as I have loved you, that you also love one another.

By this all will know that you are My disciples, if you have love for one another.

John 13:34, 35

Eternity

And this is the testimony: that God has given us eternal life, and this life is in His Son.

I John 5:11

Most assuredly, I say to you, he who hears My word and believes in Him who sent Me has everlasting life, and shall not come into judgment, but has passed from death into life.

John 5:24

For God so loved the world that He gave His only begotten Son, that whoever believes in Him should not perish but have everlasting life.

John 3:16

Most assuredly, I say to you, he who believes in Me has everlasting life.

John 6:47

And we know that the Son of God has come and has given us an understanding, that we may know Him who is true; and we are in Him who is true, in His Son Jesus Christ. This is the true God and eternal life.

I John 5:20

I am the living bread which came down from heaven. If anyone eats of this bread, he will live forever; and the bread that I shall give is My flesh, which I shall give for the life of the world.

John 6:51

The poor shall eat and be satisfied;
Those who seek Him will praise the LORD.
Let your heart live forever!

Psalm 22:26

The LORD knows the days of the upright,
And their inheritance shall be forever.

Psalm 37:18

Surely goodness and mercy shall follow me
All the days of my life;
And I will dwell in the house of the LORD
Forever.

Psalm 23:6

But God will redeem my soul from the power of the grave,
For He shall receive me. Selah

Psalm 49:15

So when this corruptible has put on incorruption, and this mortal has put on immortality, then shall be brought to pass the saying that is written: "Death is swallowed up in victory."

"O Death, where is your sting?
O Hades, where is your victory?"

I Corinthians 15:54, 55

Jesus said to her, "I am the resurrection and the life. He who believes in Me, though he may die, he shall live.

"And whoever lives and believes in me shall never die. Do you believe this?"

John 11:25, 26

Do not labor for the food which perishes, but for the food which endures to everlasting life, which the Son of Man will give you, because God the Father has set His seal on Him.

John 6:27

My sheep hear My voice, and I know them, and they follow Me.

And I give them eternal life, and they shall never perish; neither shall anyone snatch them out of My hand.

John 10:27, 28

But whoever drinks of the water that I shall give him will never thirst. But the water that I shall give him will become in him a fountain of water springing up into everlasting life.

John 4:14

Praise

This people I have formed for Myself;
They shall declare My praise.

Isaiah 43:21

But you are a chosen generation, a royal priesthood, a holy nation, His own special people, that
you may proclaim the praises of Him who called
you out of darkness into His marvelous light.

I Peter 2:9

Therefore by Him let us continually offer
the sacrifice of praise to God, that is, the fruit of
our lips, giving thanks to His name.

Hebrews 13:15

Praise the LORD! For it is good to sing praises
to our God;
For it is pleasant, and praise is beautiful.

Psalm 147:1

I will call upon the LORD, who is worthy to
be praised;
So shall I be saved from my enemies.

II Samuel 22:4

I will bless the LORD at all times;
His praise shall continually be in my mouth.

Psalm 34:1

Oh, clap your hands, all you peoples!
Shout to God with the voice of triumph!
Sing praises to God, sing praises!
Sing praises to our King, sing praises!
For God is the King of all the earth;
Sing praises with understanding.

Psalm 47:1, 6, 7

Great is the LORD, and greatly to be praised
In the city of our God,
In His holy mountain.

Psalm 48:1

Whoever offers praise glorifies Me;
And to him who orders his conduct aright
I will show the salvation of God."

Psalm 50:23

Because Your lovingkindness is better than
life,
My lips shall praise you.
Thus I will bless You while I live;

I will lift up my hands in Your name.
My soul shall be satisfied as with marrow and
fatness,
And my mouth shall praise You with joyful lips.
Psalm 63:3–5

Let my mouth be filled with Your praise
And with Your glory all the day.
But I will hope continually,
And will praise You yet more and more.
Psalm 71:8, 14

It is good to give thanks to the LORD,
And to sing praises to Your name, O Most High.
Psalm 92:1

For the LORD is great and greatly to be praised.
Psalm 96:4a

Oh, that men would give thanks to the LORD
for His goodness,
And for His wonderful works to the children
of men!

Psalm 107:8

But at midnight Paul and Silas were praying
and singing hymns to God, and the prisoners were
listening to them.

Acts 16:25

Serving God

You shall walk after the LORD your God and fear Him, and keep His commandments and obey His voice; you shall serve Him and hold fast to Him.

Deuteronomy 13:4

No one can serve two masters; for either he will hate the one and love the other, or else he will be loyal to the one and despise the other. You cannot serve God and mammon.

Matthew 6:24

Then Jesus said to him, "Away with you, Satan! For it is written, 'You shall worship the LORD your God, and Him only you shall serve.'"

Matthew 4:10

But take careful heed to do the commandment and the law which Moses the servant of the LORD commanded you, to love the LORD your God, to walk in all His ways, to keep His commandments, to hold fast to Him, and to serve Him with all your heart and with all your soul.

Joshua 22:5

I beseech you therefore, brethren, by the mercies of God, that you present your bodies a living sacrifice, holy, acceptable to God, which is your reasonable service.

And do not be conformed to this world, but be transformed by the renewing of your mind, that you may prove what is that good and acceptable and perfect will of God.

Romans 12:1, 2

Be kindly affectionate to one another with brotherly love, in honor giving preference to one another;

not lagging in diligence, fervent in spirit, serving the Lord;

distributing to the needs of the saints, given to hospitality.

Romans 12:10, 11, 13

As for you, my son Solomon, know the God of your father, and serve Him with a loyal heart and with a willing mind; for the LORD searches all hearts and understands all the intent of the thoughts. If you seek Him, He will be found by you; but if you forsake Him, He will cast you off forever.

I Chronicles 28:9

And now, Israel, what does the LORD your God require of you, but to fear the LORD your God, to walk in all His ways and to love Him, to serve the LORD your God with all your heart and with all your soul.

Deuteronomy 10:12

And it shall be that if you earnestly obey My commandments which I command you today, to love the LORD your God and serve Him with all your heart and with all your soul,

then I will give you the rain for your land in its season, the early rain and the latter rain, that you may gather in your grain, your new wine, and your oil.

And I will send grass in your fields for your livestock, that you may eat and be filled.

Deuteronomy 11:13–15

And if it seems evil to you to serve the LORD, choose for yourselves this day whom you will serve, whether the gods which your fathers served that were on the other side of the River, or the gods of the Amorites, in whose land you dwell. But as for me and my house, we will serve the LORD.

Joshua 24:15

Then Samuel said to the people, "Do not fear. You have done all this wickedness; yet do not turn aside from following the LORD, but serve the LORD with all your heart.

"And do not turn aside; for then you would go after empty things which cannot profit or deliver, for they are nothing.

"For the LORD will not forsake His people, for His great name's sake, because it has pleased the LORD to make you His people."

I Samuel 12:20–22

But now we have been delivered from the law, having died to what we were held by, so that we should serve in the newness of the Spirit and not in the oldness of the letter.

Romans 7:6

Make a joyful shout to the LORD, all you lands!
Serve the LORD with gladness;
Come before His presence with singing.
Enter into His gates with thanksgiving,
And into His courts with praise.
Be thankful to Him, and bless His name.

Psalm 100:1, 2, 4

So you shall serve the LORD your God, and He will bless your bread and your water. And I will take sickness away from the midst of you.

No one shall suffer miscarriage or be barren in your land; I will fulfill the number of your days.

Exodus 23:25, 26

Obedience

Behold, I set before you today a blessing and a curse:

the blessing, if you obey the commandments of the LORD your God which I command you today;

and the curse, if you do not obey the commandments of the LORD your God, but turn aside from the way which I command you today, to go after other gods which you have not known.

Deuteronomy 11:26–28

So Samuel said:

"Has the LORD as great delight in burnt offerings and sacrifices,
As in obeying the voice of the LORD?
Behold, to obey is better than sacrifice,
And to heed than the fat of rams."

I Samuel 15:22

Oh, that you had heeded My commandments!
Then your peace would have been like a river,
And your righteousness like the waves of the sea.

Isaiah 48:18

But this is what I commanded them, saying, "Obey My voice, and I will be your God, and you shall be My people. And walk in all the ways that I have commanded you, that it may be well with you."

Jeremiah 7:23

If you love Me, keep My commandment.

He who has My commandments and keeps them, it is he who loves Me. And he who loves Me will be loved by My Father, and I will love him and manifest Myself to him.

John 14:15, 21

But Peter and the other apostles answered and said: "We ought to obey God rather than men."

Acts 5:29

Now by this we know that we know Him, if we keep His commandments.

He who says, "I know Him," and does not keep His commandments, is a liar, and the truth is not in him.

But whoever keeps His word, truly the love of God is perfected in him. By this we know that we are in Him.

He who says he abides in Him ought himself also to walk just as He walked.

I John 2:3–6

So if you walk in My ways, to keep My statutes and My commandments, as your father David walked, then I will lengthen your days."

I Kings 3:14

Teach me to do Your will,
For You are my God;
Your Spirit is good.
Lead me in the land of uprightness.

Psalm 143:10

And Moses called all Israel, and said to them: "Hear, O Israel, the statutes and judgments which I speak in your hearing today, that you may learn them and be careful to observe them.

"Therefore you shall be careful to do as the LORD your God has commanded you; you shall not turn aside to the right hand or to the left.

"You shall walk in all the ways which the LORD your God has commanded you, that you may live and that it may be well with you, and that you may prolong your days in the land which you shall possess."

Deuteronomy 5:1, 32, 33

Bondservants, obey in all things your masters according to the flesh, not with eyeservice, as menpleasers, but in sincerity of heart, fearing God.

And whatever you do, do it heartily, as to the Lord and not to men,

knowing that from the Lord you will receive the reward of the inheritance; for you serve the Lord Christ.

Colossians 3:22–24

Therefore submit yourselves to every ordinance of man for the Lord's sake, whether to the king as supreme,

or to governors, as to those who are sent by him for the punishment of evildoers and for the praise of those who do good.

For this is the will of God, that by doing good you may put to silence the ignorance of foolish men—

as free, yet not using liberty as a cloak for vice, but as bondservants of God.

Honor all people. Love the brotherhood. Fear God. Honor the king.

Servants, be submissive to your masters with all fear, not only to the good and gentle, but also to the harsh.

For this is commendable, if because of conscience toward God one endures grief, suffering wrongfully.

For what credit is it if, when you are beaten

for your faults, you take it patiently? But when you do good and suffer, if you take it patiently, this is commendable before God.

I Peter 2:13–20

Children, obey your parents in the Lord, for this is right.

Ephesians 6:1

Children, obey your parents in all things, for this is well pleasing to the Lord.

Fathers, do not provoke your children, lest they become discouraged.

Bondservants, obey in all things your masters according to the flesh, not with eyeservice, as men-pleasers, but in sincerity of heart, fearing God.

And whatever you do, do it heartily, as to the Lord and not to men,

knowing that from the Lord you will receive the reward of the inheritance; for you serve the Lord Christ.

Colossians 3:20–24

The Carnal Mind

For to be carnally minded is death, but to be spiritually minded is life and peace.

Because the carnal mind is enmity against God; for it is not subject to the law of God, nor indeed can be.

So then, those who are in the flesh cannot please God.

Romans 8:6–8

For he who sows to his flesh will of the flesh reap corruption, but he who sows to the Spirit will of the Spirit reap everlasting life.

Galatians 6:8

Adulterers and adulteresses! Do you not know that friendship with the world is enmity with God? Whoever therefore wants to be a friend of the world makes himself an enemy of God.

James 4:4

There is a way that seems right to a man,
But its end is the way of death.

Proverbs 14:12

For many walk, of whom I have told you often, and now tell you even weeping, that they are the enemies of the cross of Christ:

whose end is destruction, whose god is their belly, and whose glory is in their shame—who set their mind on earthly things.

Philippians 3:18–19

But she who lives in pleasure is dead while she lives.

I Timothy 5:6

No one engaged in warfare entangles himself with the affairs of this life, that he may please him who enlisted him as a soldier.

Flee also youthful lusts; but pursue right-eousness, faith, love, peace with those who call on the LORD out of a pure heart.

II Timothy 2:4, 22

For men will be lovers of themselves, lovers of money, boasters, proud, blasphemers, disobedi-ent to parents, unthankful, unholy,

unloving, unforgiving, slanderers, without self-control, brutal, despisers of good,

traitors, headstrong, haughty, lovers of pleas-ure rather than lovers of God, having a form of godliness but denying its power. And from such people turn away!

For of this sort are those who creep into households and make captives of gullible women loaded down with sins, led away by various lusts,

always learning and never able to come to the knowledge of the truth.

II Timothy 3:2–7

Beloved, I beg you as sojourners and pilgrims, abstain from fleshly lusts which war against the soul.

I Peter 2:11

Do not love the world or the things in the world. If anyone loves the world, the love of the Father is not in him.

For all that is in the world—the lust of the flesh, the lust of the eyes, and the pride of life—is not of the Father but is of the world.

And the world is passing away, and the lust of it; but he who does the will of God abides forever.

I John 2:15–17

I beseech you therefore, brethren, by the mercies of God, that you present your bodies a living sacrifice, holy, acceptable to God, which is your reasonable service.

And do not be conformed to this world, but

be transformed by the renewing of your mind, that you may prove what is that good and acceptable and perfect will of God.

Romans 12:1, 2

Let this mind be in you which was also in Christ Jesus.

Philippians 2:5

You will keep him in perfect peace, whose mind is stayed on You,
Because he trusts in You.

Isaiah 26:3

Set your mind on things above, not on things on the earth.

Therefore put to death your members which are on the earth: fornication, uncleanness, passion, evil desire, and covetousness, which is idolatry.

Colossians 3:2, 5

Finally, brethren, whatever things are true, whatever things are noble, whatever things are just, whatever things are pure, whatever things are lovely, whatever things are of good report, if there is any virtue and if there is anything praiseworthy—meditate on these things.

Philippians 4:8

The Grace of God

And with great power the apostles gave witness to the resurrection of the Lord Jesus. And great grace was upon them all.

Acts 4:33

And so find favor and high esteem
In the sight of God and man.

Proverbs 3:4

For the LORD God is a sun and shield;
The LORD will give grace and glory;
No good thing will He withhold
From those who walk uprightly.

Psalm 84:11

So the LORD said to Moses, "I will also do this thing that you have spoken; for you have found grace in My sight, and I know you by name."

Exodus 33:17

You have granted me life and favor,
And Your care has preserved my spirit.

Job 10:12

For You, O LORD, will bless the righteous;
With favor You will surround him as with a
shield.

Psalm 5:12

LORD, by Your favor You have made my mountain stand strong;
You hid Your face, and I was troubled.

Psalm 30:7

The LORD has been mindful of us;
He will bless us;
He will bless the house of Israel;
He will bless the house of Aaron.
He will bless those who fear the LORD,
Both small and great.

Psalm 115:12, 13

For whoever finds me finds life,
And obtains favor from the LORD.

Proverbs 8:35

Blessings are on the head of the righteous,
But violence covers the mouth of the wicked.
The blessing of the LORD makes one rich,
And He adds no sorrow with it.
The fear of the wicked will come upon him,
And the desire of the righteous will be granted.

Proverbs 10:6, 22, 24

Fools mock at sin,
But among the upright there is favor.

Proverbs 14:9

The sons of foreigners shall build up your walls,
And their kings shall minister to you;
For in My wrath I struck you,
But in My favor I have had mercy on you.

Isaiah 60:10

For all things are for your sakes, that grace, having spread through the many, may cause thanksgiving to abound to the glory of God.

II Corinthians 4:15

To the praise of the glory of His grace, by which He made us accepted in the Beloved.

Ephesians 1:6

Let us therefore come boldly to the throne of grace, that we may obtain mercy and find grace to help in time of need.

Hebrews 4:16

The Holy Spirit

Or do you not know that your body is the temple of the Holy Spirit who is in you, whom you have from God, and you are not your own?

I Corinthians 6:19

Now hope does not disappoint, because the love of God has been poured out in our hearts by the Holy Spirit who was given to us.

Romans 5:5

And I will pray the Father, and He will give you another Helper, that He may abide with you forever—

the Spirit of truth, whom the world cannot receive, because it neither sees Him nor knows Him; but you know Him, for He dwells with you and will be in you.

John 14:16, 17

Nevertheless I tell you the truth. It is to your advantage that I go away; for if I do not go away, the Helper will not come to you; but if I depart, I will send Him to you.

However, when He, the Spirit of truth, has

come, He will guide you into all truth; for He will not speak on His own authority, but whatever He hears He will speak; and He will tell you things to come.

John 16:7, 13

I indeed baptize you with water unto repentance, but He who is coming after me is mightier than I, whose sandals I am not worthy to carry. He will baptize you with the Holy Spirit and fire.

Matthew 3:11

He who believes in Me, as the Scripture has said, out of his heart will flow rivers of living water.

But this He spoke concerning the Spirit, whom those believing in Him would receive; for the Holy Spirit was not yet given, because Jesus was not yet glorified.

John 7:38, 39

If you then, being evil, know how to give good gifts to your children, how much more will your heavenly Father give the Holy Spirit to those who ask Him!

Luke 11:13

And it shall come to pass afterward
That I will pour out My Spirit on all flesh;
Your sons and your daughters shall prophesy,
Your old men shall dream dreams,
Your young men shall see visions.

Joel 2:28

And being assembled together with them, He commanded them not to depart from Jerusalem, but to wait for the Promise of the Father, "which," He said, "you have heard from Me;

"for John truly baptized with water, but you shall be baptized with the Holy Spirit not many days from now."

"But you shall receive power when the Holy Spirit has come upon you; and you shall be witnesses to Me in Jerusalem, and in all Judea and Samaria, and to the end of the earth."

Acts 1:4, 5, 8

And they were all filled with the Holy Spirit and began to speak with other tongues, as the Spirit gave them utterance.

Acts 2:4

Then Peter said to them, "Repent, and let every one of you be baptized in the name of Jesus

Christ for the remission of sins; and you shall receive the gift of the Holy Spirit."

Acts 2:38

And when they had prayed, the place where they were assembled together was shaken; and they were all filled with the Holy Spirit, and they spoke the word of God with boldness.

Acts 4:31

And do not be drunk with wine, in which is dissipation; but be filled with the Spirit.

Ephesians 5:18

Now when the apostles who were at Jerusalem heard that Samaria had received the word of God, they sent Peter and John to them,

who, when they had come down, prayed for them that they might receive the Holy Spirit.

For as yet He had fallen upon none of them. They had only been baptized in the name of the Lord Jesus.

Then they laid hands on them, and they received the Holy Spirit.

Acts 8:14–17

While Peter was still speaking these words, the Holy Spirit fell upon all those who heard the word.

And those of the circumcision who believed were astonished, as many as came with Peter, because the gift of the Holy Spirit had been poured out on the Gentiles also.

For they heard them speak with tongues and magnify God.

Acts 10:44–46a

He said to them, "Did you receive the Holy Spirit when you believed?" So they said to him, "We have not so much as heard whether there is a Holy Spirit."

And he said to them, "Into what then were you baptized?" So they said, "Into John's baptism."

Then Paul said, "John indeed baptized with a baptism of repentance, saying to the people that they should believe on Him who would come after him, that is, on Christ Jesus."

When they heard this, they were baptized in the name of the Lord Jesus.

And when Paul had laid hands on them, the Holy Spirit came upon them, and they spoke with tongues and prophesied.

Acts 19:2–6

God's Faithfulness

You have dealt well with Your servant,
O LORD, according to Your word.

Psalm 119:65

He who calls you is faithful, who also will do it.

I Thessalonians 5:24

For this is like the waters of Noah to Me;
For as I have sworn
That the waters of Noah would no longer cover
the earth,
So have I sworn
That I would not be angry with you, nor rebuke
you.
For the mountains shall depart
And the hills be removed,
But My kindness shall not depart from you,
Nor shall My covenant of peace be removed,"
Says the LORD, who has mercy on you.

Isaiah 54:9, 10

The rainbow shall be in the cloud, and I will
look on it to remember the everlasting covenant
between God and every living creature of all
flesh that is on the earth.

Genesis 9:16

Behold, I am with you and will keep you wherever you go, and will bring you back to this land; for I will not leave you until I have done what I have spoken to you.

Genesis 28:15

But because the LORD loves you, and because He would keep the oath which He swore to your fathers, the LORD has brought you out with a mighty hand, and redeemed you from the house of bondage, from the hand of Pharaoh king of Egypt. Therefore know that the LORD your God, He is God, the faithful God who keeps covenant and mercy for a thousand generations with those who love Him and keep His commandments.

Deuteronomy 7:8, 9

Behold, this day I am going the way of all the earth. And you know in all your hearts and in all your souls that not one thing has failed of all the good things which the LORD your God spoke concerning you. All have come to pass for you; not one word of them has failed.

Joshua 23:14

Blessed be the LORD, who has given rest to His people Israel, according to all that He promised. There has not failed one word of all His good promise, which He promised through His servant Moses.

I Kings 8:56

Your mercy, O LORD, is in the heavens;
Your faithfulness reaches to the clouds.

Psalm 36:5

I will sing of the mercies of the LORD forever;
With my mouth will I make known Your faithfulness to all generations.
For I have said, "Mercy shall be built up forever;
"Your faithfulness You shall establish in the very heavens
"Nevertheless My lovingkindness I will not utterly take from him,
"Nor allow my faithfulness to fail.
"My covenant I will not break,
"Nor alter the word that has gone out of My lips."

Psalm 89:1, 2, 33, 34

He will not allow your foot to be moved;
He who keeps you will not slumber.
Behold, He who keeps Israel
Shall neither slumber nor sleep.

Psalm 121:3, 4

God is faithful, by whom you were called into the fellowship of His Son, Jesus Christ our LORD.

I Corinthians 1:9

No temptation has overtaken you except such as is common to man; but God is faithful, who will not allow you to be tempted beyond what you are able, but with the temptation will also make the way of escape, that you may be able to bear it.

I Corinthians 10:13

The LORD is not slack concerning His promise, as some count slackness, but is longsuffering toward us, not willing that any should perish but that all should come to repentance.

II Peter 3:9

If we are faithless,
He remains faithful;
He cannot deny Himself.
Nevertheless the solid foundation of God stands, having this seal: "The Lord knows those who are His," and, "Let everyone who names the name of Christ depart from iniquity."

II Timothy 2:13, 19

The Church

That in the dispensation of the fullness of the times He might gather together in one all things in Christ, both which are in heaven and which are on earth—in Him.

And He put all things under His feet, and gave Him to be head over all things to the church,

which is His body, the fullness of Him who fills all in all.

Ephesians 1:10, 22–23

He has delivered us from the power of darkness and conveyed us into the kingdom of the Son of His love,

And he is the head of the body, the church, who is the beginning, the firstborn from the dead, that in all things He may have the preeminence.

Colossians 1:13, 18

He said to them, "But who do you say that I am?"

Simon Peter answered and said, "You are the Christ, the Son of the living God."

Jesus answered and said to him, "Blessed are you, Simon Bar-Jonah, for flesh and blood has not revealed this to you, but My Father who is in heaven.

"And I also say to you that you are Peter, and on this rock I will build My church, and the gates of Hades shall not prevail against it."

Matthew 16:15–18

Having been built on the foundation of the apostles and prophets, Jesus Christ Himself being the chief cornerstone,

in whom the whole building, being fitted together, grows into a holy temple in the Lord,

In whom you also are being built together for a dwelling place of God in the Spirit.

Ephesians 2:20–22

From whom the whole family in heaven and earth is named,

to Him be glory in the church by Christ Jesus to all generations, forever and ever. Amen.

Ephesians 3:15, 21

For the husband is head of the wife, as also Christ is head of the church; and He is the Savior of the body.

Therefore, just as the church is subject to Christ, so let the wives be to their own husbands in everything.

Husbands, love your wives, just as Christ also loved the church and gave Himself for her,

that He might sanctify and cleanse her with the washing of water by the word,

that He might present her to Himself a glorious church, not having spot or wrinkle or any such thing, but that she should be holy and without blemish.

For no one ever hated his own flesh, but nourishes and cherishes it, just as the Lord does the church.

Ephesians 5:23–27, 29

And you are complete in Him, who is the head of all principality and power.

and not holding fast to the Head, from whom all the body, nourished and knit together by joints and ligaments, grows with the increase that is from God.

Colossians 2:10, 19

For as we have many members in one body, but all the members do not have the same function,

so we, being many, are one body in Christ, and individually members of one another.

Romans 12:4, 5

For as the body is one and has many members, but all the members of that one body, being many, are one body, so also is Christ.

For by one Spirit we were all baptized into one body—whether Jews or Greeks, whether slaves or free—and have all been made to drink into one Spirit.

For in fact the body is not one member but many.

If the foot should say, "Because I am not a hand, I am not of the body," is it therefore not of the body?

And if the ear should say, "Because I am not an eye, I am not of the body," is it therefore not of the body?

If the whole body were an eye, where would be the hearing? If the whole were hearing, where would be the smelling?

But now God has set the members, each one of them, in the body just as He pleased.

And if they were all one member, where would the body be?

But now indeed there are many members, yet one body.

And the eye cannot say to the hand, "I have no need of you"; nor again the head to the feet, "I have no need of you."

No, much rather, those members of the body which seem to be weaker are necessary.

And those members of the body which we think to be less honorable, on these we bestow greater honor; and our unpresentable parts have greater modesty,

but our presentable parts have no need. But God composed the body, having given greater honor to that part which lacks it,

that there should be no schism in the body, but that the members should have the same care for one another.

And if one member suffers, all the members suffer with it; or if one member is honored, all the members rejoice with it.

Now you are the body of Christ, and members individually.

And God has appointed these in the church: first apostles, second prophets, third teachers, after that miracles, then gifts of healings, helps, administrations, varieties of tongues.

I Corinthians 12:12–28

And we urge you, brethren, to recognize those who labor among you, and are over you in the Lord and admonish you, and to esteem them very highly in love for their work's sake. Be at peace among yourselves.

I Thessalonians 5:12, 13

Remember those who rule over you, who have spoken the word of God to you, whose faith follow, considering the outcome of their conduct.

Obey those who rule over you, and be submissive, for they watch out for your souls, as those who must give account. Let them do so with joy and not with grief, for that would be unprofitable for you.

Hebrews 13:7, 17

And He Himself gave some to be apostles, some prophets, some evangelists, and some pastors and teachers,

for the equipping of the saints for the work of ministry, for the edifying of the body of Christ.

Ephesians 4:11, 12

Then those who gladly received his word were baptized; and that day about three thousand souls were added to them.

And they continued steadfastly in the apostles' doctrine and fellowship, in the breaking of bread, and in prayers.

Then fear came upon every soul, and many wonders and signs were done through the apostles.

Now all who believed were together, and had all things in common,

and sold their possessions and goods, and divided them among all, as anyone had need.

So continuing daily with one accord in the temple, and breaking bread from house to house, they ate their food with gladness and simplicity of heart,

praising God and having favor with all the people. And the Lord added to the church daily those who were being saved.

Acts 2:41–47

Behold, how good and how pleasant it is
For brethren to dwell together in unity!
Psalm 133:1

Stewardship

Will a man rob God?
Yet you have robbed Me!
But you say, "In what way have we robbed You?"
In tithes and offerings.
You are cursed with a curse,
For you have robbed Me,
Even this whole nation.
Bring all the tithes into the storehouse,
That there may be food in My house,
And try Me now in this,"
Says the LORD of hosts,
"If I will not open for you the windows of heaven
And pour out for you such blessing
That there will not be room enough to receive it.
And I will rebuke the devourer for your sakes,
So that he will not destroy the fruit of your
ground,
Nor shall the vine fail to bear fruit for you in
the field,"
Says the LORD of hosts;
And all nations will call you blessed,
For you will be a delightful land,"
Says the LORD of hosts.

Malachi 3:8–12

Now concerning the collection for the saints, as I have given orders to the churches of Galatia, so you must do also:

On the first day of the week let each one of you lay something aside, storing up as he may prosper.

I Corinthians 16:1, 2a

But this I say: He who sows sparingly will also reap sparingly, and he who sows bountifully will also reap bountifully.

So let each one give as he purposes in his heart, not grudgingly or of necessity; for God loves a cheerful giver.

And God is able to make all grace abound toward you, that you, always having all sufficiency in all things, may have an abundance for every good work.

II Corinthians 9:6–8

And whatever you do, do it heartily, as to the Lord and not to men,

knowing that from the Lord you will receive the reward of the inheritance; for you serve the Lord Christ.

Colossians 3:23, 24

But lay up for yourselves treasures in heaven, where neither moth nor rust destroys and where thieves do not break in and steal.

For where your treasure is, there your heart will be also.

Matthew 6:20, 21

Give, and it will be given to you: good measure, pressed down, shaken together, and running over will be put into your bosom. For with the same measure that you use, it will be measured back to you.

Luke 6:38

Beloved, I pray that you may prosper in all things and be in health, just as your soul prospers.

III John 2

But seek first the kingdom of God and His righteousness, and all these things shall be added to you.

Matthew 6:33

And everyone who has left houses or brothers or sisters or father or mother or wife or children or lands, for My name's sake, shall receive a hundredfold, and inherit eternal life.

Matthew 19:29

Heal the sick, cleanse the lepers, raise the dead, cast out demons. Freely you have received, freely give.

Matthew 10:8

And all these blessings shall come upon you and overtake you, because you obey the voice of the LORD your God:

Blessed shall you be in the city, and blessed shall you be in the country.

Blessed shall be the fruit of your body, the produce of your ground and the increase of your herds, the increase of your cattle and the offspring of your flocks.

Blessed shall be your basket and your kneading bowl.

Blessed shall you be when you come in, and blessed shall you be when you go out.

The LORD will cause your enemies who rise against you to be defeated before your face; they shall come out against you one way and flee before you seven ways.

The LORD will command the blessing on you in your storehouses and in all to which you set your hand, and He will bless you in the land which the LORD your God is giving you.

And the LORD will grant you plenty of goods,

in the fruit of your body, in the increase of your livestock, and in the produce of your ground, in the land of which the LORD swore to your fathers to give you.

The LORD will open to you His good treasure, the heavens, to give the rain to your land in its season, and to bless all the work of your hand. You shall lend to many nations, but you shall not borrow.

Deuteronomy 28:2–8, 11, 12

Therefore keep the words of this covenant, and do them, that you may prosper in all that you do.

Deuteronomy 29:9

Then you will prosper, if you take care to fulfill the statutes and judgments with which the LORD charged Moses concerning Israel.

I Chronicles 22:13a

If they obey and serve Him,
They shall spend their days in prosperity,
And their years in pleasures.

Job 36:11

There is one who scatters, yet increases more;
And there is one who withholds more than is right,

But it leads to poverty.
The generous soul will be made rich,
And he who waters will also be watered himself.

Proverbs 11:24, 25

So Jesus answered and said, "Assuredly, I say to you, there is no one who has left house or brothers or sisters or father or mother or wife or children or lands, for My sake and the gospel's, who shall not receive a hundredfold now in this time—houses and brothers and sisters and mothers and children and lands, with persecutions—and in the age to come, eternal life."

Mark 10:29, 30

This Book of the Law shall not depart from your mouth, but you shall meditate in it day and night, that you may observe to do according to all that is written in it. For then you will make your way prosperous, and then you will have good success.

Joshua 1:8

Satan

Be sober, be vigilant; because your adversary the devil walks about like a roaring lion, seeking whom he may devour.

Resist him, steadfast in the faith.

I Peter 5:8, 9a

Therefore submit to God. Resist the devil and he will flee from you.

James 4:7

Finally, my brethren, be strong in the Lord and in the power of His might.

Put on the whole armor of God, that you may be able to stand against the wiles of the devil.

For we do not wrestle against flesh and blood, but against principalities, against powers, against the rulers of the darkness of this age, against spiritual hosts of wickedness in the heavenly places.

Therefore take up the whole armor of God, that you may be able to withstand in the evil day, and having done all, to stand.

Stand therefore, having girded your waist with truth, having put on the breastplate of righteousness, and having shod your feet with the preparation of the gospel of peace;

above all, taking the shield of faith with which you will be able to quench all the fiery darts of the wicked one.

And take the helmet of salvation, and the sword of the Spirit, which is the word of God;

praying always with all prayer and supplication in the Spirit, being watchful to this end with all perseverance and supplication for all the saints.

Ephesians 6:10–18

But we see Jesus, who was made a little lower than the angels, for the suffering of death crowned with glory and honor, that He, by the grace of God, might taste death for everyone.

Inasmuch then as the children have partaken of flesh and blood, He Himself likewise shared in the same, that through death He might destroy him who had the power of death, that is, the devil,

and release those who through fear of death were all their lifetime subject to bondage.

Hebrews 2:9, 14, 15

And you are complete in Him, who is the head of all principality and power.

Having disarmed principalities and powers, He made a public spectacle of them, triumphing over them in it.

Colossians 2:10, 15

He has delivered us from the power of darkness and conveyed us into the kingdom of the Son of His love.

Colossians 1:13

And they overcame him by the blood of the Lamb and by the word of their testimony, and they did not love their lives to the death.

Revelation 12:11

Beloved, do not believe every spirit, but test the spirits, whether they are of God; because many false prophets have gone out into the world.

By this you know the Spirit of God: Every spirit that confesses that Jesus Christ has come in the flesh is of God,

and every spirit that does not confess that Jesus Christ has come in the flesh is not of God. And this is the spirit of the Antichrist, which you have heard was coming, and is now already in the world.

You are of God, little children, and have overcome them, because He who is in you is greater
than he who is in the world.

I John 4:1–4

Then the seventy returned with joy, saying,
"Lord, even the demons are subject to us in Your
name."

And He said to them, "I saw Satan fall like
lightning from heaven.

"Behold, I give you the authority to trample
on serpents and scorpions, and over all the power
of the enemy, and nothing shall by any means
hurt you."

Luke 10:17–19

And these signs will follow those who believe:
In My name they will cast out demons; they will
speak with new tongues;

they will take up serpents; and if they drink
anything deadly, it will by no means hurt them;
they will lay hands on the sick, and they will
recover.

Mark 16:17, 18

But if I cast out demons by the Spirit of God,
surely the kingdom of God has come upon you.

Or how can one enter a strong man's house and plunder his goods, unless he first binds the strong man? And then he will plunder his house.

Matthew 12:28, 29

For though we walk in the flesh, we do not war according to the flesh.

For the weapons of our warfare are not carnal but mighty in God for pulling down strongholds,

casting down arguments and every high thing that exalts itself against the knowledge of God, bringing every thought into captivity to the obedience of Christ.

II Corinthians 10:3–5

The name of the LORD is a strong tower;
The righteous run to it and are safe.

Proverbs 18:10

He who sins is of the devil, for the devil has sinned from the beginning. For this purpose the Son of God was manifested, that He might destroy the works of the devil.

I John 3:8

And the God of peace will crush Satan under your feet shortly. The grace of our Lord Jesus Christ be with you. Amen.

Romans 16:20

I write to you, fathers,
Because you have known Him who is from
the beginning.
I write to you, young men,
Because you have overcome the wicked one.
I write to you, little children,
Because you have known the Father.
I have written to you, fathers,
Because you have known Him who is from
the beginning.
I have written to you, young men,
Because you are strong, and the word of God
abides in you,
And you have overcome the wicked one.

I John 2:13, 14

The Return of Christ

But I do not want you to be ignorant, brethren, concerning those who have fallen asleep, lest you sorrow as others who have no hope.

For if we believe that Jesus died and rose again, even so God will bring with Him those who sleep in Jesus.

For this we say to you by the word of the Lord, that we who are alive and remain until the coming of the Lord will by no means precede those who are asleep.

For the Lord Himself will descend from heaven with a shout, with the voice of an archangel, and with the trumpet of God. And the dead in Christ will rise first.

Then we who are alive and remain shall be caught up together with them in the clouds to meet the Lord in the air. And thus we shall always be with the Lord.

Therefore comfort one another with these words.

I Thessalonians 4:13–18

Behold, I tell you a mystery: We shall not all sleep, but we shall all be changed—

in a moment, in the twinkling of an eye, at the last trumpet. For the trumpet will sound, and the dead will be raised incorruptible, and we shall be changed.

For this corruptible must put on incorruption, and this mortal must put on immortality.

So when this corruptible has put on incorruption, and this mortal has put on immortality, then shall be brought to pass the saying that is written: "Death is swallowed up in victory."

"O Death, where is your sting?

O Hades, where is your victory?"

The sting of death is sin, and the strength of sin is the law.

But thanks be to God, who gives us the victory through our Lord Jesus Christ.

I Corinthians 15:51–57

Who also said, "Men of Galilee, why do you stand gazing up into heaven? This same Jesus, who was taken up from you into heaven, will so come in like manner as you saw Him go into heaven."

Acts 1:11

Looking for the blessed hope and glorious appearing of our great God and Savior Jesus Christ.

Titus 2:13

Knowing this first: that scoffers will come in the last days, walking according to their own lusts,

and saying, "Where is the promise of His coming? For since the fathers fell asleep, all things continue as they were from the beginning of creation."

But, beloved, do not forget this one thing, that with the Lord one day is as a thousand years, and a thousand years as one day.

The Lord is not slack concerning His promise, as some count slackness, but is longsuffering toward us, not willing that any should perish but that all should come to repentance.

But the day of the Lord will come as a thief in the night, in which the heavens will pass away with a great noise, and the elements will melt with fervent heat; both the earth and the works that are in it will be burned up.

Therefore, since all these things will be dissolved, what manner of persons ought you to be in holy conduct and godliness,

looking for and hastening the coming of the day of God, because of which the heavens will be dissolved, being on fire, and the elements will melt with fervent heat?

Nevertheless we, according to His promise,

look for new heavens and a new earth in which righteousness dwells.

II Peter 3:3, 4, 8–13

Beloved, now we are children of God; and it has not yet been revealed what we shall be, but we know that when He is revealed, we shall be like Him, for we shall see Him as He is.

And everyone who has this hope in Him purifies himself, just as He is pure.

I John 3:2, 3

And there will be signs in the sun, in the moon, and in the stars; and on the earth distress of nations, with perplexity, the sea and the waves roaring;

men's hearts failing them from fear and the expectation of those things which are coming on the earth, for the powers of the heavens will be shaken.

Then they will see the Son of man coming in a cloud with power and great glory.

Now when these things begin to happen, look up and lift up your heads, because your redemption draws near.

Luke 21:25–28

Now as He sat on the mount of Olives, the disciples came to Him privately, saying, "Tell us, when will these things be? And what will be the sign of Your coming, and of the end of the age?"

And Jesus answered and said to them: "Take heed that no one deceives you.

"For many will come in My name, saying, 'I am the Christ,' and will deceive many.

"And you will hear of wars and rumors of wars. See that you are not troubled; for all these things must come to pass, but the end is not yet.

"For nation will rise against nation, and kingdom against kingdom. And there will be famines, pestilences, and earthquakes in various places.

"All these are the beginning of sorrows.

"Then they will deliver you up to tribulation and kill you, and you will be hated by all nations for My name's sake.

"And then many will be offended, will betray one another, and will hate one another.

"Then many false prophets will rise up and deceive many.

"And because lawlessness will abound, the love of many will grow cold.

"But he who endures to the end shall be saved.

"And this gospel of the kingdom will be preached

in all the world as a witness to all the nations, and then the end will come."

Matthew 24:3–14

For as the lightning comes from the east and flashes to the west, so also will the coming of the Son of man be.

Immediately after the tribulation of those days the sun will be darkened, and the moon will not give its light; the stars will fall from heaven, and the powers of the heavens will be shaken.

Then the sign of the Son of man will appear in heaven, and then all the tribes of the earth will mourn, and they will see the Son of Man coming on the clouds of heaven with power and great glory.

And He will send His angels with a great sound of a trumpet, and they will gather together His elect from the four winds, from one end of heaven to the other.

Matthew 24:27, 29–31

But of that day and hour no one knows, not even the angels of heaven, but My Father only.

But as the days of Noah were, so also will the coming of the Son of Man be.

For as in the days before the flood, they were

eating and drinking, marrying and giving in marriage, until the day that Noah entered the ark,

and did not know until the flood came and took them all away, so also will the coming of the Son of Man be.

Then two men will be in the field: one will be taken and the other left.

Two women will be grinding at the mill: one will be taken and the other left.

Watch therefore, for you do not know what hour your Lord is coming.

But know this, that if the master of the house had known what hour the thief would come, he would have watched and not allowed his house to be broken into.

Therefore you also be ready, for the Son of Man is coming at an hour you do not expect.

Matthew 24:36–44

But know this, that in the last days perilous times will come:

For men will be lovers of themselves, lovers of money, boasters, proud, blasphemers, disobedient to parents, unthankful, unholy,

unloving, unforgiving, slanderers, without self-control, brutal, despisers of good,

traitors, headstrong, haughty, lovers of pleasure rather than lovers of God, having a form of godliness but denying its power. And from such people turn away!

II Timothy 3:1–5

Now the Spirit expressly says that in latter times some will depart from the faith, giving heed to deceiving spirits and doctrines of demons,

speaking lies in hypocrisy, having their own conscience seared with a hot iron,

forbidding to marry, and commanding to abstain from foods which God created to be received with thanksgiving by those who believe and know the truth.

I Timothy 4:1–3

I charge you therefore before God and the Lord Jesus Christ, who will judge the living and the dead at His appearing and His kingdom:

Preach the word! Be ready in season and out of season. Convince, rebuke, exhort, with all longsuffering and teaching.

For the time will come when they will not endure sound doctrine, but according to their own desires, because they have itching ears, they will heap up for themselves teachers;

and they will turn their ears away from the truth, and be turned aside to fables.

But you be watchful in all things, endure afflictions, do the work of an evangelist, fulfill your ministry.

For I am already being poured out as a drink offering, and the time of my departure is at hand.

I have fought the good fight, I have finished the race, I have kept the faith.

Finally, there is laid up for me the crown of righteousness, which the Lord, the righteous Judge, will give to me on that Day, and not to me only but also to all who have loved His appearing.

II Timothy 4:1–8

Assuredly, I say to you, this generation will by no means pass away till all these things take place.

Matthew 24:34

Let not your heart be troubled; you believe in God, believe also in Me.

In My Father's house are many mansions; if it were not so, I would have told you. I go to prepare a place for you.

And if I go and prepare a place for you, I will come again and receive you to Myself; that where I am, there you may be also.

And where I go you know, and the way you know.

John 14:1–4

The Unsaved

For all have sinned and fall short of the glory of God.

Romans 3:23

Therefore, just as through one man sin entered the world, and death through sin, and thus death spread to all men, because all sinned.

Romans 5:12

For the wages of sin is death, but the gift of God is eternal life in Christ Jesus our Lord.

Romans 6:23

For the wrath of God is revealed from heaven against all ungodliness and unrighteousness of men, who suppress the truth in unrighteousness,

because what may be known of God is manifest in them, for God has shown it to them.

For since the creation of the world His invisible attributes are clearly seen, being understood by the things that are made, even His eternal power and Godhead, so that they are without excuse.

Romans 1:18–20

But God demonstrates His own love toward us, in that while we were still sinners, Christ died for us.

Romans 5:8

The Lord is not slack concerning His promise, as some count slackness, but is longsuffering toward us, not willing that any should perish but that all should come to repentance.

II Peter 3:9

For God did not send His Son into the world to condemn the world, but that the world through Him might be saved.

John 3:17

I have not come to call the righteous, but sinners, to repentance.

Luke 5:32

For the Son of Man has come to seek and to save that which was lost.

Luke 19:10

Jesus answered and said to him, "Most assuredly, I say to you, unless one is born again, he cannot see the kingdom of God."

John 3:3

For God so loved the world that He gave His only begotten Son, that whoever believes in Him should not perish but have everlasting life.

John 3:16

Then they spoke the word of the Lord to him and to all who were in his house.

Acts 16:32

And He said to them, "Go into all the world and preach the gospel to every creature.

"He who believes and is baptized will be saved; but he who does not believe will be condemned."

Mark 16:15, 16

The Spirit of the LORD is upon me,
Because He has anointed Me to preach the gospel to the poor;
He has sent Me to heal the brokenhearted,
To proclaim liberty to the captives
And recovery of sight to the blind,
To set at liberty those who are oppressed;
To proclaim the acceptable year of the LORD.

Luke 4:18, 19

Truth from the Bible About...

TRUTH FROM THE BIBLE ABOUT
Forgiving Others

For if you forgive men their trespasses, your heavenly Father will also forgive you.

But if you do not forgive men their trespasses, neither will your Father forgive your trespasses.

Matthew 6:14, 15

Then Peter came to Him and said, "Lord, how often shall my brother sin against me, and I forgive him? Up to seven times?"

Jesus said to him, "I do not say to you, up to seven times, but up to seventy times seven."

Matthew 18:21, 22

Take heed to yourselves. If your brother sins against you, rebuke him; and if he repents, forgive him.

Luke 17:3

And whenever you stand praying, if you have anything against anyone, forgive him, that your Father in heaven may also forgive you your trespasses.

Mark 11:25

Bearing with one another, and forgiving one another, if anyone has a complaint against another; even as Christ forgave you, so you also must do.

Colossians 3:13

Brethren, I do not count myself to have apprehended; but one thing I do, forgetting those things which are behind and reaching forward to those things which are ahead,

I press toward the goal for the prize of the upward call of God in Christ Jesus.

Philippians 3:13, 14

Do not remember the former things,
Nor consider the things of old.
Behold, I will do a new thing,
Now it shall spring forth;
Shall you not know it?
I will even make a road in the wilderness
And rivers in the desert.

Isaiah 43:18, 19

For this is commendable, if because of conscience toward God one endures grief, suffering wrongfully.

For what credit is it if, when you are beaten

for your faults, you take it patiently? But when you do good and suffer, if you take it patiently, this is commendable before God.

For to this you were called, because Christ also suffered for us, leaving us an example, that you should follow His steps:

"Who committed no sin,
Nor was deceit found in His mouth."

who, when He was reviled, did not revile in return; when He suffered, He did not threaten, but committed Himself to Him who judges righteously.

I Peter 2:19–23

Blessed are those who are persecuted for righteousness' sake,
For theirs is the kingdom of heaven.

Blessed are you when they revile and persecute you, and say all kinds of evil against you falsely for My sake.

Rejoice and be exceedingly glad, for great is your reward in heaven, for so they persecuted the prophets who were before you.

Matthew 5:10–12

For we know Him who said, "Vengeance is Mine, I will repay," says the Lord. And again, "The LORD will judge His people."

Hebrews 10:30

Beloved, do not think it strange concerning the fiery trial which is to try you, as though some strange thing happened to you;

but rejoice to the extent that you partake of Christ's sufferings, that when His glory is revealed, you may also be glad with exceeding joy.

If you are reproached for the name of Christ, blessed are you, for the Spirit of glory and of God rests upon you. On their part He is blasphemed, but on your part He is glorified.

I Peter 4:12–14

But I say to you, love your enemies, bless those who curse you, do good to those who hate you, and pray for those who spitefully use you and persecute you.

Matthew 5:44

Do not be overcome by evil, but overcome evil with good.

Romans 12:21

Not returning evil for evil or reviling for reviling, but on the contrary blessing, knowing that you were called to this, that you may inherit a blessing.

For He who would love life
And see good days,

Let him refrain his tongue from evil,
And his lips from speaking deceit.

I Peter 3:9, 10

Let all bitterness, wrath, anger, clamor, and evil speaking be put away from you, with all malice.

And be kind to one another, tenderhearted, forgiving one another, even as God in Christ forgave you.

Ephesians 4:31, 32

TRUTH FROM THE BIBLE ABOUT
Christian Fellowship

That which we have seen and heard we declare to you, that you also may have fellowship with us; and truly our fellowship is with the Father and with His Son Jesus Christ.

But if we walk in the light as He is in the light, we have fellowship with one another, and the blood of Jesus Christ His Son cleanses us from all sin.

I John 1:3, 7

And walk in love, as Christ also has loved us and given Himself for us, an offering and a sacrifice to God for a sweet-smelling aroma.

speaking to one another in psalms and hymns and spiritual songs, singing and making melody in your heart to the Lord,

For we are members of His body, of His flesh and of His bones.

Ephesians 5:2, 19, 30

Let the word of Christ dwell in you richly in all wisdom, teaching and admonishing one another in psalms and hymns and spiritual songs, singing with grace in your hearts to the Lord.

Colossians 3:16

That their hearts may be encouraged, being knit together in love, and attaining to all riches of the full assurance of understanding, to the knowledge of the mystery of God, both of the Father and of Christ.

Colossians 2:2

Then those who feared the LORD spoke to one another,
And the LORD listened and heard them;
So a book of remembrance was written before Him
For those who fear the LORD
And who meditate on His name.

Malachi 3:16

Now behold, two of them were traveling that same day to a village called Emmaus, which was seven miles from Jerusalem.
And they talked together of all these things which had happened.
So it was, while they conversed and reasoned, that Jesus Himself drew near and went with them.

Luke 24:13–15

We took sweet counsel together,
And walked to the house of God in the throng.

Psalm 55:14

Now I am no longer in the world, but these are in the world, and I come to You. Holy Father, keep through Your name those whom You have given Me, that they may be one as We are.

that they all may be one, as You, Father, are in Me, and I in You; that they also may be one in Us, that the world may believe that You sent Me.

And the glory which You gave Me I have given them, that they may be one just as We are one:

I in them, and You in Me; that they may be made perfect in one, and that the world may know that You have sent Me, and have loved them as You have loved Me.

John 17:11, 21–23

When the Day of Pentecost had fully come, they were all with one accord in one place.

And they continued steadfastly in the apostles' doctrine and fellowship, in the breaking of bread, and in prayers.

So continuing daily with one accord in the temple, and breaking bread from house to house, they ate their food with gladness and simplicity of heart,

praising God and having favor with all the people. And the Lord added to the church daily those who were being saved.

Acts 2:1, 42, 46, 47

Now may the God of patience and comfort grant you to be like-minded toward one another, according to Christ Jesus,

that you may with one mind and one mouth glorify the God and Father of our Lord Jesus Christ.

Therefore receive one another, just as Christ also received us, to the glory of God.

Romans 15:5–7

Now I plead with you, brethren, by the name of our Lord Jesus Christ, that you all speak the same thing, and that there be no divisions among you, but that you be perfectly joined together in the same mind and in the same judgment.

I Corinthians 1:10

Bear one another's burdens, and so fulfill the law of Christ.

Therefore, as we have opportunity, let us do good to all, especially to those who are of the household of faith.

Galatians 6:2, 10

Now, therefore, you are no longer strangers and foreigners, but fellow citizens with the saints and members of the household of God,

having been built on the foundation of the apostles and prophets, Jesus Christ Himself being the chief cornerstone, in whom the whole building, being fitted together, grows into a holy temple in the Lord,

in whom you also are being built together for a dwelling place of God in the Spirit.

Ephesians 2:19–22

I thank my God upon every remembrance of you,

Only let your conduct be worthy of the gospel of Christ, so that whether I come and see you or am absent, I may hear of your affairs, that you stand fast in one spirit, with one mind striving together for the faith of the gospel.

Philippians 1:3, 27

Therefore if there is any consolation in Christ, if any comfort of love, if any fellowship of the Spirit, if any affection and mercy,

fulfill my joy by being like-minded, having the same love, being of one accord, of one mind.

Philippians 2:1, 2

And let us consider one another in order to stir up love and good works,

not forsaking the assembling of ourselves together, as is the manner of some, but exhorting one another, and so much the more as you see the Day approaching.

Hebrews 10:24, 25

Your Responsibility

And He said to them, "Go into all the world and preach the gospel to every creature."

Mark 16:15

But you shall receive power when the Holy Spirit has come upon you; and you shall be witnesses to Me in Jerusalem, and in all Judea and Samaria, and to the end of the earth.

Acts 1:8

You are the salt of the earth; but if the salt loses its flavor, how shall it be seasoned? It is then good for nothing but to be thrown out and trampled underfoot by men.

You are the light of the world. A city that is set on a hill cannot be hidden.

Nor do they light a lamp and put it under a basket, but on a lampstand, and it gives light to all who are in the house.

Let your light so shine before men, that they may see your good works and glorify your Father in heaven.

Matthew 5:13–16

For I was hungry and you gave Me food; I was thirsty and you gave Me drink; I was a stranger and you took Me in;

I was naked and you clothed Me; I was sick and you visited Me; I was in prison and you came to Me.

Then the righteous will answer Him, saying, "Lord, when did we see You hungry and feed You, or thirsty and give You drink?

When did we see You a stranger and take You in, or naked and clothe You?

Or when did we see You sick, or in prison, and come to You?"

And the King will answer and say to them, "Assuredly, I say to you, inasmuch as you did it to one of the least of these My brethren, you did it to Me."

Matthew 25:35–40

And whoever gives one of these little ones only a cup of cold water in the name of a disciple, assuredly, I say to you, he shall by no means lose his reward.

Matthew 10:42

For God is not unjust to forget your work and labor of love which you have shown toward

His name, in that you have ministered to the saints, and do minister.

Hebrews 6:10

Pure and undefiled religion before God and the Father is this: to visit orphans and widows in their trouble, and to keep oneself unspotted from the world.

James 1:27

If a brother or sister is naked and destitute of daily food,

and one of you says to them, "Depart in peace, be warmed and filled," but you do not give them the things which are needed for the body, what does it profit?

Thus also faith by itself, if it does not have works, is dead.

James 2:15–17

So the people asked him, saying, "What shall we do then?"

He answered and said to them, "He who has two tunics, let him give to him who has none; and he who has food, let him do likewise."

Luke 3:10, 11

Brethren, if a man is overtaken in any trespass, you who are spiritual restore such a one in a spirit of gentleness, considering yourself lest you also be tempted.

Bear one another's burdens, and so fulfill the law of Christ.

For if anyone thinks himself to be something, when he is nothing, he deceives himself.

But let each one examine his own work, and then he will have rejoicing in himself alone, and not in another.

For each one shall bear his own load.

Let him who is taught the word share in all good things with him who teaches.

Galatians 6:1–6

By this we know love, because He laid down His life for us. And we also ought to lay down our lives for the brethren.

But whoever has this world's goods, and sees his brother in need, and shuts up his heart from him, how does the love of God abide in him?

My little children, let us not love in word or in tongue, but in deed and in truth.

I John 3:16–18

And these words which I command you today shall be in your heart.

You shall teach them diligently to your children, and shall talk of them when you sit in your house, when you walk by the way, when you lie down, and when you rise up.

You shall bind them as a sign on your hand, and they shall be as frontlets between your eyes.

You shall write them on the doorposts of your house and on your gates.

Deuteronomy 6:6–9

But if anyone does not provide for his own, and especially for those of his household, he has denied the faith and is worse than an unbeliever.

I Timothy 5:8

Train up a child in the way he should go,
And when he is old he will not depart from it.

Proverbs 22:6

Therefore you shall lay up these words of mine in your heart and in your soul, and bind them as a sign on your hand, and they shall be as frontlets between your eyes.

You shall teach them to your children, speaking of them when you sit in your house, when you walk by the way, when you lie down, and when you rise up.

Deuteronomy 11:18, 19

Speaking God's Word

For assuredly, I say to you, whoever says to this mountain, "Be removed and be cast into the sea," and does not doubt in his heart, but believes that those things he says will be done, he will have whatever he says.

Mark 11:23

So the Lord said, "If you have faith as a mustard seed, you can say to this mulberry tree, 'Be pulled up by the roots and be planted in the sea,' and it would obey you."

Luke 17:6

Then He arose and rebuked the wind, and said to the sea, "Peace, be still!" And the wind ceased and there was a great calm.

Mark 4:39

By faith we understand that the worlds were framed by the word of God, so that the things which are seen were not made of things which are visible.

Hebrews 11:3

For I have not spoken on My own authority; but the Father who sent Me gave Me a command, what I should say and what I should speak.

And I know that His command is everlasting life. Therefore, whatever I speak, just as the Father has told Me, so I speak.

John 12:49, 50

I will raise up for them a Prophet like you from among their brethren, and will put My words in His mouth, and He shall speak to them all that I command Him.

Deuteronomy 18:18

Bless the LORD, you His angels,
Who excel in strength, who do His word,
Heeding the voice of His word.

Psalm 103:20

The wise in heart will be called prudent,
And sweetness of the lips increases learning.
The heart of the wise teaches his mouth,
And adds learning to his lips.
Pleasant words are like a honeycomb,
Sweetness to the soul and health to the bones.
An ungodly man digs up evil,
And it is on his lips like a burning fire.

He winks his eye to devise perverse things;
He purses his lips and brings about evil.

Proverbs 16:21, 23, 24, 27, 30

The words of a man's mouth are deep waters;
The wellspring of wisdom is a flowing brook.
A fool's mouth is his destruction,
And his lips are the snare of his soul.
A man's stomach shall be satisfied from the
fruit of his mouth;
From the produce of his lips he shall be filled.
Death and life are in the power of the tongue,
And those who love it will eat its fruit.

Proverbs 18:4, 7, 20, 21

For out of the abundance of the heart the
mouth speaks.
But I say to you that for every idle word men
may speak, they will give account of it in the day
of judgment.
For by your words you will be justified, and
by your words you will be condemned.

Matthew 12:34b, 36, 37

If anyone among you thinks he is religious,
and does not bridle his tongue but deceives his
own heart, this one's religion is useless.

James 1:26

But the righteousness of faith speaks in this way,

But what does it say? "The word is near you, in your mouth and in your heart" (that is, the word of faith which we preach):

that if you confess with your mouth the Lord Jesus and believe in your heart that God has raised Him from the dead, you will be saved.

For with the heart one believes unto righteousness, and with the mouth confession is made unto salvation.

Romans 10:6a, 8–10

Let us hold fast the confession of our hope without wavering, for He who promised is faithful.

Hebrews 10:23

And since we have the same spirit of faith, according to what is written, "I believed and therefore I spoke," we also believe and therefore speak.

II Corinthians 4:13

Beat your plowshares into swords
And your pruning hooks into spears;
Let the weak say, "I am strong."

Joel 3:10

A man shall eat well by the fruit of his mouth,
But the soul of the unfaithful feeds on violence.
He who guards his mouth preserves his life,
But he who opens wide his lips shall have destruction.

Proverbs 13:2, 3

There is one who speaks like the piercings of a sword,
But the tongue of the wise promotes health.

Proverbs 12:18

Finding the Will of God

If any of you lacks wisdom, let him ask of God, who gives to all liberally and without reproach, and it will be given to him.

James 1:5

I will instruct you and teach you in the way you should go;
I will guide you with My eye.

Psalm 32:8

Your word is a lamp to my feet
And a light to my path.

Psalm 119:105

When you roam, they will lead you;
When you sleep, they will keep you;
And when you awake, they will speak with you.
For the commandment is a lamp,
And the law a light;
Reproofs of instruction are the way of life.

Proverbs 6:22, 23

This Book of the Law shall not depart from your mouth, but you shall meditate in it day and night, that you may observe to do according to all that is written in it. For then you will make your way prosperous, and then you will have good success.

Joshua 1:8

Your ears shall hear a word behind you, saying,
"This is the way, walk in it,"
Whenever you turn to the right hand
Or whenever you turn to the left.

Isaiah 30:21

However, when He, the Spirit of truth, has come, He will guide you into all truth; for He will not speak on His own authority, but whatever He hears He will speak; and He will tell you things to come.

John 16:13

For this is God,
Our God forever and ever;
He will be our guide even to death.

Psalm 48:14

Commit your works to the LORD,
And your thoughts will be established.

Proverbs 16:3

The steps of a good man are ordered by the
LORD,
    And He delights in his way.

Psalm 37:23

For You are my rock and my fortress;
Therefore, for Your name's sake,
    Lead me and guide me.

Psalm 31:3

You also gave Your good spirit to instruct them,
    And did not withhold Your manna from
their mouth,
    And gave them water for their thirst.

Nehemiah 9:20

Trust in the Lord with all your heart,
And lean not on your own understanding;
In all your ways acknowledge Him,
    And He shall direct your paths.

Proverbs 3:5, 6

Thus says the LORD, your Redeemer,
The Holy One of Israel:
"I am the LORD your God,
Who teaches you to profit,
Who leads you by the way you should go."

Isaiah 48:17

Answered Prayer

It shall come to pass
That before they call, I will answer;
And while they are still speaking, I will hear.

Isaiah 65:24

Ask, and it will be given to you; seek, and you will find; knock, and it will be opened to you.

For everyone who asks receives, and he who seeks finds, and to him who knocks it will be opened.

Matthew 7:7, 8

And whatever things you ask in prayer, believing, you will receive.

Matthew 21:22

Again I say to you that if two of you agree on earth concerning anything that they ask, it will be done for them by My Father in heaven.

For where two or three are gathered together in My name, I am there in the midst of them.

Matthew 18:19, 20

And whatever you ask in My name, that I will do, that the Father may be glorified in the Son.

John 14:13

Therefore I say to you, whatever things you ask when you pray, believe that you receive them, and you will have them.

Mark 11:24

If you abide in Me, and My words abide in you, you will ask what you desire, and it shall be done for you.

John 15:7

And in that day you will ask Me nothing. Most assuredly, I say to you, whatever you ask the Father in My name He will give you.

John 16:23

Let us therefore come boldly to the throne of grace, that we may obtain mercy and find grace to help in time of need.

Hebrews 4:16

Delight yourself also in the LORD,
And He shall give you the desires of your heart.
Psalm 37:4

He shall call upon Me, and I will answer him;
I will be with him in trouble;
I will deliver him and honor him.
Psalm 91:15

The LORD is near to all who call upon Him,
To all who call upon Him in truth.
He will fulfill the desire of those who fear Him;
He also will hear their cry and save them.

Psalm 145:18, 19

The LORD is far from the wicked,
But He hears the prayer of the righteous.

Proverbs 15:29

Call to Me, and I will answer you, and show you great and mighty things, which you do not know.

Jeremiah 33:3

But you, when you pray, go into your room, and when you have shut your door, pray to your Father who is in the secret place; and your Father who sees in secret will reward you openly.

Matthew 6:6

And whatever we ask we receive from Him, because we keep His commandments and do those things that are pleasing in His sight.

I John 3:22

Unsaved Loved Ones

So they said, "Believe on the Lord Jesus Christ, and you will be saved, you and your household."

Acts 16:31

Who will tell you words by which you and all your household will be saved.

Acts 11:14

Even so it is not the will of your Father who is in heaven that one of these little ones should perish.

Matthew 18:14

For I will pour water on him who is thirsty,
And floods on the dry ground;
I will pour My Spirit on your descendants,
And My blessing on your offspring.

Isaiah 44:3

The Lord is not slack concerning His promise, as some count slackness, but is longsuffering toward us, not willing that any should perish but that all should come to repentance.

II Peter 3:9

Wives, likewise, be submissive to your own husbands, that even if some do not obey the word, they, without a word, may be won by the conduct of their wives,

when they observe your chaste conduct accompanied by fear.

I Peter 3:1, 2

And a woman who has a husband who does not believe, if he is willing to live with her, let her not divorce him.

For the unbelieving husband is sanctified by the wife, and the unbelieving wife is sanctified by the husband; otherwise your children would be unclean, but now they are holy.

But if the unbeliever departs, let him depart; a brother or a sister is not under bondage in such cases. But God has called us to peace.

For how do you know, O wife, whether you will save your husband? Or how do you know, O husband, whether you will save your wife?

I Corinthians 7:13–16

Who among you fears the LORD?
Who obeys the voice of His servant?
Who walks in darkness
And has no light?
Let him trust in the name of the LORD
And rely upon his God.

Isaiah 50:10

Test all things; hold fast what is good.
Abstain from every form of evil.

I Thessalonians 5:21, 22

The LORD has made known His salvation;
His righteousness He has revealed in the sight
of the nations.

Psalm 98:2

Cast your burden on the LORD, and He shall
sustain you; He shall never permit the righteous to
be moved.

Psalm 55:22

Thus says the LORD:
"Keep justice, and do righteousness,
For My salvation is about to come,
And My righteousness to be revealed."

Isaiah 56:1

Nevertheless I tell you the truth. It is to
your advantage that I go away; for if I do not go
away, the Helper will not come to you; but if I
depart, I will send Him to you.

And when He has come, He will convict the
world of sin, and of righteousness, and of judgment.

John 16:7, 8

Train up a child in the way he should go,
And when he is old he will not depart from it.

Proverbs 22:6

He who calls you is faithful, who also will
do it.

I Thessalonians 5:24

Marriage

And the LORD God said, "It is not good that man should be alone; I will make him a helper comparable to him."

Genesis 2:18

Therefore a man shall leave his father and mother and be joined to his wife, and they shall become one flesh.

Genesis 2:24

He who finds a wife finds a good thing,
And obtains favor from the LORD.

Proverbs 18:22

Take wives and beget sons and daughters; and take wives for your sons and give your daughters to husbands, so that they may bear sons and daughters—that you may be increased there, and not diminished.

Jeremiah 29:6

I will betroth you to Me forever;
Yes, I will betroth you to Me
In righteousness and justice,

In lovingkindness and mercy;
I will betroth you to Me in faithfulness,
And you shall know the LORD.

Hosea 2:19, 20

Nevertheless, because of sexual immorality, let each man have his own wife, and let each woman have her own husband.

Let the husband render to his wife the affection due her, and likewise also the wife to her husband.

The wife does not have authority over her own body, but the husband does. And likewise the husband does not have authority over his own body, but the wife does.

I Corinthians 7:2–4

Therefore I desire that the younger widows marry, bear children, manage the house, give no opportunity to the adversary to speak reproachfully.

I Timothy 5:14

Marriage is honorable among all, and the bed undefiled; but fornicators and adulterers God will judge.

Hebrews 13:4

Wives, submit to your own husbands, as to the Lord.

For the husband is head of the wife, as also Christ is head of the church; and He is the Savior of the body.

Therefore, just as the church is subject to Christ, so let the wives be to their own husbands in everything.

Husbands, love your wives, just as Christ also loved the church and gave Himself for her,

that He might sanctify and cleanse her with the washing of water by the word,

That He might present her to Himself a glorious church, not having spot or wrinkle or any such thing, but that she should be holy and without blemish.

So husbands ought to love their own wives as their own bodies; he who loves his wife loves himself.

For no one ever hated his own flesh, but nourishes and cherishes it, just as the Lord does the church.

For we are members of His body, of His flesh and of His bones.

"For this reason a man shall leave his father and mother and be joined to his wife, and the two shall become one flesh."

This is a great mystery, but I speak concerning Christ and the church.

Nevertheless let each one of you in particular so love his own wife as himself, and let the wife see that she respects her husband.

Ephesians 5:22–33

Wives, likewise, be submissive to your own husbands, that even if some do not obey the word, they, without a word, may be won by the conduct of their wives.

I Peter 3:1

Husbands, likewise, dwell with them with understanding, giving honor to the wife, as to the weaker vessel, and as being heirs together of the grace of life, that your prayers may not be hindered.

I Peter 3:7

Divorce

Furthermore it has been said, "Whoever divorces his wife, let him give her a certificate of divorce."

But I say to you that whoever divorces his wife for any reason except sexual immorality causes her to commit adultery; and whoever marries a woman who is divorced commits adultery.

Matthew 5:31, 32

The Pharisees also came to Him, testing Him, and saying to Him, "Is it lawful for a man to divorce his wife for just any reason?"

And He answered and said to them, "Have you not read that He who made them at the beginning 'made them male and female,'

"and said, 'For this reason a man shall leave his father and mother and be joined to his wife, and the two shall become one flesh'?

"So then, they are no longer two but one flesh. Therefore what God has joined together, let not man separate."

They said to Him, "Why then did Moses command to give a certificate of divorce, and to put her away?"

He said to them, "Moses, because of the hardness of your hearts, permitted you to divorce your wives, but from the beginning it was not so.

"And I say to you, whoever divorces his wife, except for sexual immorality, and marries another, commits adultery; and whoever marries her who is divorced commits adultery."

Matthew 19:3–9

The Pharisees came and asked Him, "Is it lawful for a man to divorce his wife?" testing Him.

And He answered and said to them, "What did Moses command you?"

They said, "Moses permitted a man to write a certificate of divorce, and to dismiss her."

And Jesus answered and said to them, "Because of the hardness of your heart he wrote you this precept.

"But from the beginning of the creation, God 'made them male and female.'

"'For this reason a man shall leave his father and mother and be joined to his wife,

"And the two shall become one flesh'; so then they are no longer two, but one flesh.

"Therefore what God has joined together, let not man separate."

In the house His disciples also asked Him again about the same matter.

So He said to them, "Whoever divorces his wife and marries another commits adultery against her.

"And if a woman divorces her husband and marries another, she commits adultery."

Mark 10:2–12

Whoever divorces his wife and marries another commits adultery; and whoever marries her who is divorced from her husband commits adultery.

Luke 16:18

Now to the married I command, yet not I but the Lord: A wife is not to depart from her husband.

But even if she does depart, let her remain unmarried or be reconciled to her husband. And a husband is not to divorce his wife.

But to the rest I, not the Lord, say: If any brother has a wife who does not believe, and she is willing to live with him, let him not divorce her.

And a woman who has a husband who does not believe, if he is willing to live with her, let her not divorce him.

For the unbelieving husband is sanctified by the wife, and the unbelieving wife is sanctified by the husband; otherwise your children would be unclean, but now they are holy.

But if the unbeliever departs, let him depart; a brother or a sister is not under bondage in such cases. But God has called us to peace.

For how do you know, O wife, whether you will save your husband? Or how do you know, O husband, whether you will save your wife?

But as God has distributed to each one, as the Lord has called each one, so let him walk. And so I ordain in all the churches.

I Corinthians 7:10–17

When a man takes a wife and marries her, and it happens that she finds no favor in his eyes because he has found some uncleanness in her, and he writes her a certificate of divorce, puts it in her hand, and sends her out of his house,

when she has departed from his house, and goes and becomes another man's wife,

if the latter husband detests her and writes her a certificate of divorce, puts it in her hand, and sends her out of his house, or if the latter husband dies who took her as his wife,

then her former husband who divorced her must not take her back to be his wife after she has been defiled; for that is an abomination before the LORD, and you shall not bring sin on the land which the LORD your God is giving you as an inheritance.

Deuteronomy 24:1–4

"They say, 'If a man divorces his wife,
And she goes from him
And becomes another man's,
May he return to her again?'
Would not that land be greatly polluted?
But you have played the harlot with many lovers;
Yet return to Me," says the LORD.

Jeremiah 3:1

Your Family

So they said, "Believe on the Lord Jesus Christ, and you will be saved, you and your household."

Acts 16:31

And if it seems evil to you to serve the LORD, choose for yourselves this day whom you will serve, whether the gods which your fathers served that were on the other side of the River, or the gods of the Amorites, in whose land you dwell. But as for me and my house, we will serve the LORD."

Joshua 24:15

Let all bitterness, wrath, anger, clamor, and evil speaking be put away from you, with all malice.

And be kind to one another, tenderhearted, forgiving one another, even as God in Christ forgave you.

Ephesians 4:31, 32

Train up a child in the way he should go,
And when he is old he will not depart from it.

Proverbs 22:6

Honor your father and your mother, that your days may be long upon the land which the LORD your God is giving you.

Exodus 20:12

Submitting to one another in the fear of God.

Wives, submit to your own husbands, as to the Lord.

For the husband is head of the wife, as also Christ is head of the church; and He is the Savior of the body.

Therefore, just as the church is subject to Christ, so let the wives be to their own husbands in everything.

Husbands, love your wives, just as Christ also loved the church and gave Himself for her,

that He might sanctify and cleanse her with the washing of water by the word,

that He might present her to Himself a glorious church, not having spot or wrinkle or any such thing, but that she should be holy and without blemish.

So husbands ought to love their own wives as their own bodies; he who loves his wife loves himself.

For no one ever hated his own flesh, but nourishes and cherishes it, just as the Lord does the church.

For we are members of His body, of His flesh and of His bones.

"For this reason a man shall leave his father and mother and be joined to his wife, and the two shall become one flesh."

This is a great mystery, but I speak concerning Christ and the church.

Nevertheless let each one of you in particular so love his own wife as himself, and let the wife see that she respects her husband.

Children, obey your parents in the Lord, for this is right.

"Honor your father and mother," which is the first commandment with promise:

"That it may be well with you and you may live long on the earth."

And you, fathers, do not provoke your children to wrath, but bring them up in the training and admonition of the Lord.

Ephesians 5:21–6:4

One who rules his own house well, having his children in submission with all reverence

(for if a man does not know how to rule his own house, how will he take care of the church of God?).

I Timothy 3:4, 5

Behold, children are a heritage from the LORD,
The fruit of the womb is a reward.
Like arrows in the hand of a warrior,
So are the children of one's youth.
Happy is the man who has his quiver full of
them;
They shall not be ashamed,
But shall speak with their enemies in the gate.

Psalm 127:3–5

And he will turn
The hearts of the fathers to the children,
And the hearts of the children to their fathers,
Lest I come and strike the earth with a curse.

Malachi 4:6

Children's children are the crown of old men,
And the glory of children is their father.

Proverbs 17:6

And these words which I command you today
shall be in your heart.

You shall teach them diligently to your children, and shall talk of them when you sit in your
house, when you walk by the way, when you lie
down, and when you rise up.

You shall bind them as a sign on your hand,
and they shall be as frontlets between your eyes.

You shall write them on the doorposts of your house and on your gates.

Deuteronomy 6:6–9

Correct your son, and he will give you rest;
Yes, he will give delight to your soul.

Proverbs 29:17

And you, fathers, do not provoke your children to wrath, but bring them up in the training and admonition of the Lord.

Ephesians 6:4

A good man leaves an inheritance to his children's children,
But the wealth of the sinner is stored up for the righteous.

Proverbs 13:22

Blessed is every one who fears the LORD,
Who walks in His ways.
When you eat the labor of your hands,
You shall be happy, and it shall be well with you.
Your wife shall be like a fruitful vine in the very heart of your house,
Your children like olive plants
All around your table.

Behold, thus shall the man be blessed
Who fears the LORD.

Psalm 128:1–4

The father of the righteous will greatly rejoice,
And he who begets a wise child will delight in him.

Proverbs 23:24

All your children shall be taught by the LORD,
And great shall be the peace of your children.

Isaiah 54:13

Wives

He who finds a wife finds a good thing,
And obtains favor from the Lord.

Proverbs 18:22

Wives, likewise, be submissive to your own husbands, that even if some do not obey the word, they, without a word, may be won by the conduct of their wives,

when they observe your chaste conduct accompanied by fear.

Do not let your adornment be merely outward—arranging the hair, wearing gold, or putting on fine apparel—

rather let it be the hidden person of the heart, with the incorruptible beauty of a gentle and quiet spirit, which is very precious in the sight of God.

For in this manner, in former times, the holy women who trusted in God also adorned themselves, being submissive to their own husbands,

as Sarah obeyed Abraham, calling him lord, whose daughters you are if you do good and are not afraid with any terror.

Husbands, likewise, dwell with them with understanding, giving honor to the wife, as to the weaker vessel, and as being heirs together of the grace of life, that your prayers may not be hindered.

I Peter 3:1–7

Live joyfully with the wife whom you love all the days of your vain life which He has given you under the sun, all your days of vanity; for that is your portion in life, and in the labor which you perform under the sun.

Ecclesiastes 9:9

Let the husband render to his wife the affection due her, and likewise also the wife to her husband.

I Corinthians 7:3

Let your fountain be blessed,
And rejoice with the wife of your youth.
As a loving deer and a graceful doe,
Let her breasts satisfy you at all times;
And always be enraptured with her love.

Proverbs 5:18, 19

Wives, submit to your own husbands, as is fitting in the Lord.

Colossians 3:18

Your wife shall be like a fruitful vine
In the very heart of your house,

Your children like olive plants
All around your table.

Psalm 128:3

Submitting to one another in the fear of God.

Wives, submit to your own husbands, as to the Lord.

For the husband is head of the wife, as also Christ is head of the church; and He is the Savior of the body.

Therefore, just as the church is subject to Christ, so let the wives be to their own husbands in everything.

Husbands, love your wives, just as Christ also loved the church and gave Himself for her,

that He might sanctify and cleanse her with the washing of water by the word,

that He might present her to Himself a glorious church, not having spot or wrinkle or any such thing, but that she should be holy and without blemish.

So husbands ought to love their own wives as their own bodies; he who loves his wife loves himself.

For no one ever hated his own flesh, but nourishes and cherishes it, just as the Lord does the church.

For we are members of His body, of His flesh and of His bones.

"For this reason a man shall leave his father and mother and be joined to his wife, and the two shall become one flesh."

This is a great mystery, but I speak concerning Christ and the church.

Nevertheless let each one of you in particular so love his own wife as himself, and let the wife see that she respects her husband.

Ephesians 5:21–33

Who can find a virtuous wife?
For her worth is far above rubies.
The heart of her husband safely trusts her;
So he will have no lack of gain.
She does him good and not evil
All the days of her life.
She seeks wool and flax,
And willingly works with her hands.
She is like the merchant ships,
She brings her food from afar.
She also rises while it is yet night,
And provides food for her household,
And a portion for her maidservants.
She considers a field and buys it;
From her profits she plants a vineyard.

She girds herself with strength,
And strengthens her arms.
She perceives that her merchandise is good,
And her lamp does not go out by night.
She stretches out her hands to the distaff,
And her hand holds the spindle.
She extends her hand to the poor,
Yes, she reaches out her hands to the needy.
She is not afraid of snow for her household,
For all her household is clothed with scarlet.
She makes tapestry for herself;
Her clothing is fine linen and purple.
Her husband is known in the gates,
When he sits among the elders of the land.
She makes linen garments and sells them,
And supplies sashes for the merchants.
Strength and honor are her clothing;
She shall rejoice in time to come.
She opens her mouth with wisdom,
And on her tongue is the law of kindness.
She watches over the ways of her household,
And does not eat the bread of idleness.
Her children rise up and call her blessed;
Her husband also, and he praises her:
"Many daughters have done well,
But you excel them all."
Charm is deceitful and beauty is passing,

But a woman who fears the LORD, she shall be praised.
Give her of the fruit of her hands,
And let her own works praise her in the gates.
Proverbs 31:10–31

An excellent wife is the crown of her husband,
But she who causes shame is like rottenness in his bones.

Proverbs 12:4

The wise woman builds her house,
But the foolish pulls it down with her hands.
Proverbs 14:1

Houses and riches are an inheritance from fathers,
But a prudent wife is from the LORD.
Proverbs 19:14

TRUTH FROM THE BIBLE ABOUT
Widows

Pure and undefiled religion before God and the Father is this: to visit orphans and widows in their trouble, and to keep oneself unspotted from the world.

James 1:27

The blessing of a perishing man came upon me,
And I caused the widow's heart to sing for joy.
Job 29:13

He administers justice for the fatherless and the widow, and loves the stranger, giving him food and clothing.

Deuteronomy 10:18

The LORD will destroy the house of the proud,
But he will establish the boundary of the widow.
Proverbs 15:25

The LORD watches over the strangers;
He relieves the fatherless and widow;
But the way of the wicked He turns upside down.

Psalm 146:9

Leave your fatherless children,
I will preserve them alive;
And let your widows trust in Me.

Jeremiah 49:11

For your Maker is your husband,
The Lord of hosts is his name;
And your Redeemer is the Holy One of Israel;
He is called the God of the whole earth.

Isaiah 54:5

A wife is bound by law as long as her husband lives; but if her husband dies, she is at liberty to be married to whom she wishes, only in the Lord.

But she is happier if she remains as she is, according to my judgment—and I think I also have the Spirit of God.

I Corinthians 7:39, 40

He heals the brokenhearted
And binds up their wounds.

Psalm 147:3

A father of the fatherless, a defender of widows,
Is God in His holy habitation.

Psalm 68:5

I will not leave you orphans; I will come to you.

John 14:18

Cursed is the one who perverts the justice due the stranger, the fatherless, and widow.
And all the people shall say, "Amen!"

Deuteronomy 27:19

Therefore by Him let us continually offer the sacrifice of praise to God, that is, the fruit of our lips, giving thanks to His name.

Hebrews 13:15

Teaching them to observe all things that I have commanded you; and lo, I am with you always, even to the end of the age. Amen.

Matthew 28:20

Therefore you now have sorrow; but I will see you again and your heart will rejoice, and your joy no one will take from you.

John 16:22

Singles

I will betroth you to Me forever;
Yes, I will betroth you to Me
In righteousness and justice,
In lovingkindness and mercy.

Hosea 2:19

But I say to the unmarried and to the widows:
It is good for them if they remain even as I am.

I Corinthians 7:8

But as God has distributed to each one, as the
Lord has called each one, so let him walk. And so
I ordain in all the churches.

I Corinthians 7:17

Are you bound to a wife? Do not seek to be
loosed. Are you loosed from a wife? Do not seek a
wife.

But even if you do marry, you have not
sinned; and if a virgin marries, she has not
sinned. Nevertheless such will have trouble in
the flesh, but I would spare you.

I Corinthians 7:27, 28

But I want you to be without care. He who
is unmarried cares for the things of the Lord—
how he may please the Lord.

But he who is married cares about the things of the world—how he may please his wife.

And this I say for your own profit, not that I may put a leash on you, but for what is proper, and that you may serve the Lord without distraction.

I Corinthians 7:32, 33, 35

Nevertheless he who stands steadfast in his heart, having no necessity, but has power over his own will, and has so determined in his heart that he will keep his virgin, does well.

I Corinthians 7:37

Marriage is honorable among all, and the bed undefiled; but fornicators and adulterers God will judge.

Hebrews 13:4

Trust in the LORD with all your heart,
And lean not on your own understanding;
In all your ways acknowledge Him,
And He shall direct your paths.

Proverbs 3:5, 6

Delight yourself also in the LORD,
And He shall give you the desires of your heart.

Psalm 37:4

Therefore, my brethren, you also have become dead to the law through the body of Christ, that you may be married to another—to Him who was raised from the dead, that we should bear fruit to God.

Romans 7:4

But let each one examine his own work, and then he will have rejoicing in himself alone, and not in another.

Galatians 6:4

To knowledge self-control, to self-control perseverance, to perseverance godliness,
to godliness brotherly kindness, and to brotherly kindness love.
For if these things are yours and abound, you will be neither barren nor unfruitful in the knowledge of our Lord Jesus Christ.

II Peter 1:6–8

The Elderly

Even to your old age, I am He,
And even to gray hairs I will carry you!
I have made, and I will bear;
Even I will carry, and will deliver you.

Isaiah 46:4

O God, You have taught me from my youth;
And to this day I declare Your wondrous works.
Now also when I am old and grayheaded,
O God, do not forsake me,
Until I declare Your strength to this generation,
Your power to everyone who is to come.

Psalm 71:17, 18

The glory of young men is their strength,
And the splendor of old men is their gray head.

Proverbs 20:29

The silver-haired head is a crown of glory,
If it is found in the way of righteousness.

Proverbs 16:31

They shall still bear fruit in old age;
They shall be fresh and flourishing.

Psalm 92:14

For length of days and long life
And peace they will add to you.

Proverbs 3:2

With long life I will satisfy him,
And show him my salvation.

Psalm 91:16

I have been young, and now am old;
Yet I have not seen the righteous forsaken,
Nor his descendants begging bread.

Psalm 37:25

Let your conduct be without covetousness; be content with such things as you have. For He Himself has said, "I will never leave you nor forsake you."

Hebrews 13:5

For what is our hope, or joy, or crown of rejoicing? Is it not even you in the presence of our Lord Jesus Christ at His coming?

I Thessalonians 2:19

Yea, though I walk through the valley of the shadow of death,
I will fear no evil;

For You are with me;
Your rod and Your staff, they comfort me.

Psalm 23:4

The poor and needy seek water, but there is none,
Their tongues fail for thirst.
I, the LORD, will hear them;
I, the God of Israel, will not forsake them.

Isaiah 41:17

Because you would forget your misery,
And remember it as waters that have passed away.

Job 11:16

Why are you cast down, O my soul?
And why are you disquieted within me?
Hope in God, for I shall yet praise Him
For the help of His countenance.

Psalm 42:5

For I am persuaded that neither death nor life,
Nor angels nor principalities nor powers, nor things present nor things to come,
nor height nor depth, nor any other created

thing, shall be able to separate us from the love of
God which is in Christ Jesus our Lord.

Romans 8:38, 39

For since the beginning of the world
Men have not heard nor perceived by the
ear,
Nor has the eye seen any God besides You,
Who acts for the one who waits for Him.

Isaiah 64:4

Surely goodness and mercy shall follow me
All the days of my life;
And I will dwell in the house of the LORD
Forever.

Psalm 23:6

What You Can Do to...

Grow Spiritually

But grow in the grace and knowledge of our Lord and Savior Jesus Christ. To Him be the glory both now and forever. Amen.

II Peter 3:18

As newborn babes, desire the pure milk of the word, that you may grow thereby,

if indeed you have tasted that the Lord is gracious.

I Peter 2:2, 3

Be diligent to present yourself approved to God, a worker who does not need to be ashamed, rightly dividing the word of truth.

II Timothy 2:15

Meditate on these things; give yourself entirely to them, that your progress may be evident to all.

I Timothy 4:15

Therefore, leaving the discussion of the elementary principles of Christ, let us go on to perfection.

Hebrews 6:1a

But also for this very reason, giving all diligence, add to your faith virtue, to virtue knowledge,

to knowledge self-control, to self-control perseverance, to perseverance godliness,

to godliness brotherly kindness, and to brotherly kindness love.

For if these things are yours and abound, you will be neither barren nor unfruitful in the knowledge of our Lord Jesus Christ.

II Peter 1:5–8

For this reason I bow my knees to the Father of our Lord Jesus Christ,

from whom the whole family in heaven and earth is named,

that He would grant you, according to the riches of His glory, to be strengthened with might through His Spirit in the inner man,

that Christ may dwell in your hearts through faith; that you, being rooted and grounded in love,

may be able to comprehend with all the saints what is the width and length and depth and height—

to know the love of Christ which passes knowledge; that you may be filled with all the fullness of God.

Ephesians 3:14–19

For this reason we also, since the day we heard it, do not cease to pray for you, and to ask that you may be filled with the knowledge of His will in all wisdom and spiritual understanding;

that you may walk worthy of the Lord, fully pleasing him, being fruitful in every good work and increasing in the knowledge of God;

strengthened with all might, according to His glorious power, for all patience and longsuffering with joy.

Colossians 1:9–11

Let the word of Christ dwell in you richly in all wisdom, teaching and admonishing one another in psalms and hymns and spiritual songs, singing with grace in your hearts to the Lord.

Colossians 3:16

But we all, with unveiled face, beholding as in a mirror the glory of the Lord, are being transformed into the same image from glory to glory, just as by the Spirit of the Lord.

II Corinthians 3:18

The righteous shall flourish like a palm tree,
He shall grow like a cedar in Lebanon.

Psalm 92:12

Being confident of this very thing, that He who has begun a good work in you will complete it until the day of Jesus Christ;

And this I pray, that your love may abound still more and more in knowledge and all discernment,

that you may approve the things that are excellent, that you may be sincere and without offense till the day of Christ.

Philippians 1:6, 9, 10

That we should no longer be children, tossed to and fro and carried about with every wind of doctrine, by the trickery of men, in the cunning craftiness of deceitful plotting,

but, speaking the truth in love, may grow up in all things into Him who is the head—Christ.

Ephesians 4:14, 15

Change the World

You are the light of the world. A city that is set on a hill cannot be hidden.

Nor do they light a lamp and put it under a basket, but on a lampstand, and it gives light to all who are in the house.

Let your light so shine before men, that they may see your good works and glorify your Father in heaven.

Matthew 5:14–16

Those who are wise shall shine like the brightness of the firmament, and those who turn many to righteousness like the stars forever and ever.

Daniel 12:3

And He said to them, "Go into all the world and preach the gospel to every creature.

"He who believes and is baptized will be saved; but he who does not believe will be condemned.

"And these signs will follow those who believe: In My name they will cast out demons; they will speak with new tongues;

"they will take up serpents; and if they drink anything deadly, it will by no means hurt them;

they will lay hands on the sick, and they will recover."

So then, after the Lord had spoken to them, He was received up into heaven, and sat down at the right hand of God.

And they went out and preached everywhere, the Lord working with them and confirming the word through the accompanying signs. Amen.

Mark 16:15–20

But you shall receive power when the Holy Spirit has come upon you; and you shall be witnesses to Me in Jerusalem, and in all Judea and Samaria, and to the end of the earth.

Acts 1:8

The Spirit of the LORD is upon Me,
Because He has anointed Me to preach the gospel to the poor;
He has sent Me to heal the brokenhearted,
To proclaim liberty to the captives
And recovery of sight to the blind,
To set at liberty those who are oppressed.

Luke 4:18

Most assuredly, I say to you, he who believes in Me, the works that I do he will do also; and greater works than these he will do, because I go to My Father.

John 14:12

And I also say to you that you are Peter, and on this rock I will build my church, and the gates of Hades shall not prevail against it.

And I will give you the keys of the kingdom of heaven, and whatever you bind on earth will be bound in heaven, and whatever you loose on earth will be loosed in heaven.

Matthew 16:18, 19

A new commandment I give to you, that you love one another; as I have loved you, that you also love one another.

By this all will know that you are My disciples, if you have love for one another.

John 13:34, 35

We are of God. He who knows God hears us; he who is not of God does not hear us. By this we know the spirit of truth and the spirit of error.

And we have known and believed the love that God has for us. God is love, and he who abides in love abides in God, and God in him.

Love has been perfected among us in this: that we may have boldness in the day of judgment; because as He is, so are we in this world.

I John 4:6, 16, 17

For whatever is born of God overcomes the world. And this is the victory that has overcome the world—our faith.

Who is he who overcomes the world, but he who believes that Jesus is the Son of God?

I John 5:4, 5

Now faith is the substance of things hoped for, the evidence of things not seen.

For by it the elders obtained a good testimony.

By faith we understand that the worlds were framed by the word of God, so that the things which are seen were not made of things which are visible.

who through faith subdued kingdoms, worked righteousness, obtained promises, stopped the mouths of lions,

quenched the violence of fire, escaped the edge of the sword, out of weakness were made strong, became valiant in battle, turned to flight the armies of the aliens.

Hebrews 11:1–3, 33, 34

You are the salt of the earth.

Matthew 5:13a

For God so loved the world that He gave His only begotten Son, that whoever believes in Him should not perish but have everlasting life.

John 3:16

Go therefore and make disciples of all the nations, baptizing them in the name of the Father and of the Son and of the Holy Spirit,
teaching them to observe all things that I have commanded you; and lo, I am with you always, even to the end of the age. Amen.

Matthew 28:19, 20

Help Your Business

This Book of the Law shall not depart from your mouth, but you shall meditate in it day and night, that you may observe to do according to all that is written in it. For then you will make your way prosperous, and then you will have good success.

Joshua 1:8

Thus says the LORD, your Redeemer,
The Holy One of Israel:
"I am the LORD your God,
Who teaches you to profit,
Who leads you by the way you should go."

Isaiah 48:17

Beloved, I pray that you may prosper in all things and be in health, just as your soul prospers.

III John 2

And you shall remember the LORD your God, for it is He who gives you power to get wealth, that he may establish His covenant which He swore to your fathers, as it is this day.

Deuteronomy 8:18

Trust in the LORD with all your heart,
And lean not on your own understanding;
In all your ways acknowledge Him,
And He shall direct your paths.
Do not be wise in your own eyes;
Fear the LORD and depart from evil.
It will be health to your flesh,
And strength to your bones.
Honor the LORD with your possessions,
And with the firstfruits of all your increase;
So your barns will be filled with plenty,
And your vats will overflow with new wine.

Proverbs 3:5–10

Then you will prosper, if you take care to fulfill the statutes and judgments with which the LORD charged Moses concerning Israel. Be strong and of good courage; do not fear nor be dismayed.

I Chronicles 22:13

Blessed is the man
Who walks not in the counsel of the ungodly,
Nor stands in the path of sinners,
Nor sits in the seat of the scornful;
But his delight is in the law of the LORD,
And in His law he meditates day and night.

He shall be like a tree
Planted by the rivers of water,
That brings forth its fruit in its season,
Whose leaf also shall not wither;
And whatever he does shall prosper.

Psalm 1:1–3

Now it shall come to pass, if you diligently obey the voice of the LORD your God, to observe carefully all His commandments which I command you today, that the LORD your God will set you high above all nations of the earth.

And all these blessings shall come upon you and overtake you, because you obey the voice of the LORD your God:

"Blessed shall you be in the city, and blessed shall you be in the country.

"Blessed shall be the fruit of your body, the produce of your ground and the increase of your herds, the increase of your cattle and the offspring of your flocks.

"Blessed shall be your basket and your kneading bowl.

"Blessed shall you be when you come in, and blessed shall you be when you go out.

"The LORD will command the blessing on you in your storehouses and in all to which you set your hand, and He will bless you in the land which the LORD your God is giving you.

"And the LORD will grant you plenty of goods, in the fruit of your body, in the increase of your livestock, and in the produce of your ground, in the land of which the LORD swore to your fathers to give you.

"The LORD will open to you His good treasure, the heavens, to give the rain to your land in its season, and to bless all the work of your hand. You shall lend to many nations, but you shall not borrow.

"And the LORD will make you the head and not the tail; you shall be above only, and not be beneath, if you heed the commandments of the LORD your God, which I command you today, and are careful to observe them."

Deuteronomy 28:1–6, 8, 11–13

But seek first the kingdom of God and His righteousness, and all these things shall be added to you.

Matthew 6:33

Commit your works to the LORD,
And your thoughts will be established.

Proverbs 16:3

Through wisdom a house is built,
And by understanding it is established;
By knowledge the rooms are filled
With all precious and pleasant riches.

Proverbs 24:3, 4

I go the way of all the earth; be strong, therefore, and prove yourself a man.

And keep the charge of the LORD your God: to walk in His ways, to keep His statutes, His commandments, His judgments, and His testimonies, as it is written in the Law of Moses, that you may prosper in all that you do and wherever you turn.

I Kings 2:2, 3

If they obey and serve Him,
They shall spend their days in prosperity,
And their years in pleasures.

Job 36:11

Not lagging in diligence, fervent in spirit, serving the Lord.

Romans 12:11

Masters, give your bondservants what is just and fair, knowing that you also have a Master in heaven.

Colossians 4:1

Please God

Everyone who is called by My name,
Whom I have created for My glory;
I have formed him, yes, I have made him.
This people I have formed for Myself;
They shall declare My praise.

Isaiah 43:7, 21

But the hour is coming, and now is, when the true worshipers will worship the Father in spirit and truth; for the Father is seeking such to worship Him.

God is Spirit, and those who worship Him must worship in spirit and truth.

John 4:23, 24

Indeed it came to pass, when the trumpeters and singers were as one, to make one sound to be heard in praising and thanking the LORD, and when they lifted up their voice with the trumpets and cymbals and instruments of music, and praised the LORD, saying:

"For He is good,
For His mercy endures forever,"

That the house, the house of the LORD, was filled with a cloud, so that the priests could not continue ministering because of the cloud; for the glory of the LORD filled the house of God.

II Chronicles 5:13, 14

You also, as living stones, are being built up a spiritual house, a holy priesthood, to offer up spiritual sacrifices acceptable to God through Jesus Christ.

But you are a chosen generation, a royal priesthood, a holy nation, His own special people, that you may proclaim the praises of Him who called you out of darkness into His marvelous light.

I Peter 2:5, 9

Therefore by Him let us continually offer the sacrifice of praise to God, that is, the fruit of our lips, giving thanks to His name.

But do not forget to do good and to share, for with such sacrifices God is well pleased.

Hebrews 13:15, 16

You are worthy, O Lord,
To receive glory and honor and power;
For You created all things,
And by Your will they exist and were created.

Revelation 4:11

But without faith it is impossible to please Him, for he who comes to God must believe that He is, and that He is a rewarder of those who diligently seek him.

Hebrews 11:6

That you may walk worthy of the Lord, fully pleasing Him, being fruitful in every good work and increasing in the knowledge of God.

Colossians 1:10

I beseech you therefore, brethren, by the mercies of God, that you present your bodies a living sacrifice, holy, acceptable to God, which is your reasonable service.

And do not be conformed to this world, but be transformed by the renewing of your mind, that you may prove what is that good and acceptable and perfect will of God.

Romans 12:1, 2

Therefore I exhort first of all that supplications, prayers, intercessions, and giving of thanks be made for all men,

For this is good and acceptable in the sight of God our Savior.

I desire therefore that the men pray everywhere, lifting up holy hands, without wrath and doubting.

I Timothy 2:1, 3, 8

My mouth shall speak the praise of the LORD,
And all flesh shall bless His holy name
Forever and ever.

Psalm 145:21

I will greatly praise the LORD with my mouth;
Yes, I will praise Him among the multitude.

Psalm 109:30

Oh, clap your hands, all you peoples!
Shout to God with the voice of triumph!

Psalm 47:1

The LORD takes pleasure in those who fear Him,
In those who hope in His mercy.

Psalm 147:11

Praise the Lord!
Sing to the LORD a new song,
And His praise in the assembly of saints.
Let Israel rejoice in their Maker;
Let the children of Zion be joyful in their King.

Let them praise His name with the dance;
Let them sing praises to Him with the timbrel and harp.
For the LORD takes pleasure in His people;
He will beautify the humble with salvation.
Let the saints be joyful in glory;
Let them sing aloud on their beds.
Let the high praises of God be in their mouth.

Psalm 149:1–6a

So then, those who are in the flesh cannot please God.
But you are not in the flesh but in the Spirit.

Romans 8:8, 9a

And whatever we ask we receive from Him, because we keep His commandments and do those things that are pleasing in His sight.

I John 3:22

God's Plan of
Salvation...

GOD'S PLAN OF
Salvation

Therefore, just as through one man sin entered the world, and death through sin, and thus death spread to all men, because all sinned.

Romans 5:12

For all have sinned and fall short of the glory of God.

Romans 3:23

For the wages of sin is death, but the gift of God is eternal life in Christ Jesus our Lord.

Romans 6:23

But God demonstrates His own love toward us, in that while we were still sinners, Christ died for us.

Romans 5:8

Moreover, brethren, I declare to you the gospel which I preached to you, which also you received and in which you stand,
by which also you are saved, if you hold fast that word which I preached to you—unless you believed in vain.

For I delivered to you first of all that which I also received: that Christ died for our sins according to the Scriptures,

and that He was buried, and that He rose again the third day according to the Scriptures.

I Corinthians 15:1–4

For God did not send His Son into the world to condemn the world, but that the world through Him might be saved.

John 3:17

He who believes in the Son has everlasting life; and he who does not believe the Son shall not see life, but the wrath of God abides on him.

John 3:36

For God so loved the world that He gave His only begotten Son, that whoever believes in Him should not perish but have everlasting life.

John 3:16

But as many as received Him, to them he gave the right to become children of God, to those who believe in His name.

John 1:12

For by grace you have been saved through faith, and that not of yourselves; it is the gift of God, not of works, lest anyone should boast.

Ephesians 2:8, 9

Behold, I stand at the door and knock. If anyone hears My voice and opens the door, I will come in to him and dine with him, and he with Me.

Revelation 3:20

But what does it say? "The word is near you, in your mouth and in your heart" (that is, the word of faith which we preach):

that if you confess with your mouth the Lord Jesus and believe in your heart that God has raised Him from the dead, you will be saved.

For with the heart one believes unto righteousness, and with the mouth confession is made unto salvation.

Romans 10:8–10

Therefore whoever confesses Me before men, him I will also confess before My Father who is in heaven.

Matthew 10:32

And this is the testimony: that God has given us eternal life, and this life is in His Son.

He who has the Son has life; he who does not have the Son of God does not have life.

These things I have written to you who believe in the name of the Son of God, that you may know that you have eternal life, and that you may continue to believe in the name of the Son of God.

I John 5:11–13

MY PRAYER LIST

_____

_____

_____

_____

_____

_____

_____

_____

_____

_____

_____

_____

_____

_____

_____

_____

_____

_____

_____

_____

_____

_____

_____

_____

MY PRAYER LIST

MY PRAYER LIST

MY PRAYER LIST

_____

_____

_____

_____

_____

_____

_____

_____

_____

_____

_____

_____

_____

_____

_____

_____

_____

_____

_____

_____

_____

_____

_____

_____

MY PRAYER LIST

_____

_____

_____

_____

_____

_____

_____

_____

_____

_____

_____

_____

_____

_____

_____

_____

_____

_____

_____

_____

_____

_____

_____

_____

_____

PERSONAL STUDY NOTES

PERSONAL STUDY NOTES

PERSONAL STUDY NOTES

PERSONAL STUDY NOTES

PERSONAL STUDY NOTES

PERSONAL STUDY NOTES

_____

_____

_____

_____

_____

_____

_____

_____

_____

_____

_____

_____

_____

_____

_____

_____

_____

_____

_____

_____

_____

_____

_____

_____